THE
AMBIVALENT
MEMOIRIST

Obsessions Digressions Epiphanies

SANDRA HURTES

In various places in the book, names were changed to protect the privacy of the individuals.

For my family

THANK YOU

*T*he *Ambivalent Memoirist* began as a blog, "Finding My Place Through Writing and Teaching." I owe a huge thank-you to my readers who showed up on Day One and urged me to keep going. I'm grateful to my gifted editor, Sheila Bender, for showing me the difference between a blog and a book and helping me get there. Elizabeth Smith is more than a copyeditor; her early read was instrumental in story development. Thank you to Anita Salzberg for insightful comments and writerly support. I'm grateful to my cousins Vera Feldman and Joan Mandelkehr for their love and support of my writer's life.

"There are experiences I shy away from.
But my curiosity, creativeness,
urge me beyond these boundaries,
to transcend my character."

~Anaïs Nin

Choices—A Prologue

I began working as a writer in 1995, when I was forty-four years old. I held an assortment of temporary jobs as a secretary, proofreader, and substitute teacher. In the mornings and evenings, I wrote and sent out essays and articles to newspapers and magazines.

Early in my career, the *New York Times* published my essay "Keeping Alive the Dreams of Love." The story about my brief romance with a man I'd met ballroom dancing created a bit of a stir with agents and editors. They called and wrote to me, asking if I had a book-length manuscript they could read. (I didn't.) And then there was a book packager who asked me to partner with him to write a novel. He asked me to think it over.

I wanted to write a novel, but my idea of how to do that was banging out word after word after word with nobody looking over my shoulder and maybe a glass of something chilled and tingly nearby, to fill in the spaces between words.

Working with the book packager would have cost me nothing but time, but I told him no. I said I was certain and went to work on my novel *Knitting Lessons*; I worked on it on and off for seven years. The manuscript now lives rent-free on a shelf in my closet right next to three versions of a memoir I never completed. The packager? Well . . .

there *was* a cover article about him and two doctors-turned-writers in the *New York Times Magazine* several years ago. They teamed up and wrote a novel together. They sold it for millions. Millions!

Who's to know? When I second-guess myself (and I do), I feel that I should have said yes. Actually, yes!

But I'm not a "yes" person. I ponder, sift, reflect, and wait.

I lived then in a stately apartment building on a quiet block in Brooklyn Heights. I moved to the neighborhood in 1977 from the Ditmas section of Brooklyn. I wanted to be close to my friend Ann and also to put some distance between myself and my parents, whom I'd had a difficult time separating from. I had really wanted to move to Manhattan; but Brooklyn's edge was as far as I could get. The broken land that was once called Breuckelen held my family's history in every crack. That history was so deep, it reached beneath the Atlantic Ocean and back.

In 1947, two years after their liberation from Nazi concentration camps, my parents found refuge in the East New York section of Brooklyn. Their homes in Czechoslovakia destroyed, they'd had no place to return to. And so they came to America, where my father's sister lived. She helped my parents set up their first home together. On Pitkin Avenue and later, in Crown Heights, they formed a clan of Holocaust survivors that remained intact their entire lives. They spoke broken English in thick accents; their voices rose and fell, dramatic and heavy on the ground, *v*'s and *w*'s transposed, *r*'s rippled through the air, like *sveet-hearrrt* and *rrraining*.

Brooklyn was the place, too, that my mother's five sisters and brothers, survivors every one, came to, one family at a time, from Israel. They settled near us in Crown Heights; every Friday night we walked to one apartment building where my mother's three sisters and their families lived.

Brooklyn soil. Rife with thick, gnarly accents and high-pitched emotions that peaked into the air then fell heavy upon the earth. Those sounds and feelings had reverberated within me from the moment I was born in 1950, three years after my brother, Lenny. The woman who shared my mother's room at Brooklyn Women's Hospital and gave birth on the same day was an Auschwitz survivor, like my mother. Their delirium over their second babies fell upon my tender ears, slid into my pores. Brooklyn was an emotional patchwork and I was sewn into its seams.

I remember the day in 1977 when I drove with my parents to see my new apartment in Brooklyn Heights, an hour drive from where they then lived in Flatlands. I was twenty-six, divorced, and although I loved to write, I had no hopes that I could actually make such a life happen. I was a traditional Jewish girl; I had married young, had expected to have children and bring my parents happiness. But I'd been too young to leave my parents, too young to know how to treat love.

BROOKLYN BOUND

M y parents and I were in their silver-green Chevy Impala. We wound around the Brooklyn Queens Expressway. My mother and I puffed on our Kents, while she held back tears. My father turned right at Cadman Plaza, Brooklyn's last exit, and we circled a winding street to get to my new apartment.

"Where are you moving?" my mother asked, her eyes red and wrenching behind her oversize sunglasses. She suffered from ringing in the ears and wore a kerchief over her golden-blonde hair to protect herself from the wind. With her Hungarian accent she held a strong resemblance to the Gabor sisters. Her name was Ava, but everyone called her Zsa Zsa.

"It's Brooklyn Heights, you'll see. It's beautiful here," I tried consoling her. I don't believe she or my father had heard of the neighborhood until then.

"This is beautiful? This is old. I came from old," my mother said, when she saw the landmark brownstones and prewar building I was moving into.

I don't recall what she thought of my one-bedroom rental. But I do remember needing her approval, needing her to feel at home in this new "old" world, an hour's drive from their apartment. We went out for lunch to Piccadilly's, a restaurant that served the best shrimp salad sandwiches. My mother loved seafood, Chinese food, bacon, ham, everything non-kosher we didn't eat at home.

By the end of that day, her world opened a bit, and Brooklyn Heights was, perhaps, not as distant as it had seemed. To clinch the deal, I presented her with a set of keys. So, maybe it was my fault that my parents went shopping the next day for shelf paper, thumbtacks, kitchen towels, assorted knickknacks. Maybe it was my fault that without telling me, they went back to my apartment, gave the super two hundred dollars to keep an eye on me, took the elevator to the ninth floor, let themselves in with their keys while I was at work, and filled my refrigerator and pantry, papered my linen closet shelves, organized my sheets, toiletries, and towels.

I remember walking into the apartment as my parents scurried through the closets like mice, smiling nervously when I turned on them wide-eyed.

"What are you doing here?"

"What do you mean, 'What are we doing here'?" my mother said. "We're making it easy for you!"

"You can't just come here without telling me!"

"What's such a big deal," my father said. "It's a closet. It's nothing."

It's not nothing! I cried to myself.

"I'm sorry, *Símala*," my mother said, addressing me as she always did, in the diminutive of my Hebrew name, *Sima*. "We'll never do it again." Her eyes watered, her face seemed to melt.

My parents gathered their supplies: clothes hangers, a feather duster, a bottle of Lysol, handi-wipes. Their shopping bags, traveling stores like the Lower East Side pushcarts of long ago, would be toted back to their apartment.

"At least take the hammer and scissors," my mother pleaded. "You'll need them."

"I have scissors. A hammer, too. This isn't my first apartment."

"Take them, please. I couldn't find scissors in your house anywhere."

I took the scissors and put them in a drawer. When my parents left, I emptied the linen closet and considered ripping off the floral paper. I imagine I lifted the pinking-sheared edge, then felt the thumb-tacks' pull. More than likely my fingers lingered midair, contemplating what to do, as they would do in the twenty-seven years I lived in that apartment.

I tried throwing everything away, even a tapestry from Czechoslovakia of lovebirds in muted purples and greens. And yet, a few weeks later, I took the tapestry of the birds to a local frame shop. I hung the black oval frame in my living room, opposite a cuckoo clock my mother had given me that also came from Czechoslovakia.

S oon after moving, I found a job at a small advertising agency on 48th Street and Madison Avenue as a receptionist. Before that I was a secretary at the Crown Heights public school I'd attended. I loved the crazy energy of Midtown Manhattan—traffic, pedestrians, ad agencies like BBDO and Ogilvy and Maher on every corner; Simon and Schuster was down the block. Rizzoli Books, Classic Bookshop, and Scribner's devoured my lunch and after-work hours. I found a fantastic clothing store, the Emotional Outlet, near the Museum of Modern Art. Midtown was my center of the world.

One evening, my friend Ann and I wandered along Broadway and lingered at Lincoln Center; then we wound our way to 72nd Street and the subway.

"I'd love to live up here," I said, looking around awestruck. Across the street, people crowded in front of Papaya King. The ABC television studios were a few blocks away. The air was crisp; every corner filled with possibility.

Ann's eyes opened wide; she shook her head. "Would your parents let you?"

I didn't react to the preposterousness of that statement, because I didn't feel it as such. Not because I *couldn't* move, but because a life of free choice hadn't been ordained for me. I knew that instinctively; that knowledge was the thread that had sewn me together.

Ann and I took the subway home. In our respective apartments, Ann worked on her doctoral dissertation, and I took baby steps toward being a writer. The first sentence I wrote was: *When I caught my mother smuggling three boxes of strawberries, a cantaloupe, and a bunch of grapes she had hidden under her blouse into my refrigerator I was out of control.* The written words were my grasp at autonomy.

I settled into Brooklyn Heights. I dated a lot; my relationships lasted from three months to two years. Then I met Ken, who was twenty-five years older than I, with two divorces behind him. We lasted five years. Only in hindsight did I realize we were ill suited from the start.

The years went by. I went back to school and earned my bachelor's degree. My parents didn't often ask about my romantic life, but they desperately wanted a grandchild. They felt isolated from their peers whose children were married and having babies.

I still wanted the life I'd envisioned when I'd stood in front of Papaya King with Ann. When my apartment building turned co-op and offered tenants an insider price of twenty thousand dollars, I wanted to run. My parents, Ken, and everyone else I knew thought that I'd be insane to walk away. My parents begged, "Please let us help you. You can buy two apartments." I thought, *No. God no!* My mother noted the shock on my face, said, "Don't worry. We're not going to live with you." The best I could do was say yes to "buying" the apartment I lived in and, mercifully, I said no to buying two.

Then I settled further into a life where my yeses and nos were all mixed up.

When I look back now to 1977, more than thirty years gone by, I recall that in that moment in front of Papaya King, Ann and I were two young women on the brink of everything—although Ann was a "yes" person and I was a "no." I gazed across a Manhattan I wanted to inhabit. Not doing so was a turning point that didn't turn.

And when I look back to 1983 when I "bought" my apartment, I see a slightly older version of the same woman still unable to reach for what she wanted. When the book packager called in 1996 about my essay in the *New York Times*, that was my chance to make everything right. I could have made a bundle of money, left Brooklyn Heights, gone to Hollywood, where my novel might have been turned into a screenplay (and then . . . well . . . maybe won an Academy Award).

But I hadn't said yes to that chance. I wasn't friends with Ann by then but wondered if she'd seen my name in the *Times*. I wanted to tell her I finally began the writing career that had been bubbling inside of me. I didn't want to tell her I still lived in Brooklyn.

In 2002 I went to my first writers' conference in Cape Cod. The conference grounds in Hyannis were bleached and spectacular. There was a beach on one side, a bay on the other. Mornings, I walked along a floral-scented path to the dining hall, past pastel homes with boats docked out back. Swans floated by, regal and breathtaking. I wondered, *Where have I been my whole life?*

I took my journal to the beach, sat on the cool sand; I felt let loose from something strong and visceral. I wrote: *It is not enough to have insights. If I want to move forward in my life, at some point I must be in motion.*

One year later, my Zsa Zsa Gabor mother died of heart disease. She was seventy-six. Her death sent me so low, my feet tangled up in the roots beneath Brooklyn's soil, even though my mother was buried in Florida. When my grief subsided, the extraordinary longing for life that she had carried encompassed me. I brushed off the dirt, rose up through the earth.

I sold my co-op. The chorus around me said: *Invest in another apartment. If you're going to move, move some place! Go to California. Go to Hawaii.*

I did go someplace.

On March 16, 2004, I crossed the Brooklyn Bridge, for every one of its metaphoric and literal meanings.

A Last Good-bye

Manhattan is now my home. But today, I look over my shoulder at the Brooklyn that raised me. I look into an obscure distance and wonder, am I where I belong?

My former neighbor Rick is moving after thirty-two years in his Brooklyn Heights apartment. He's found his place in Palm Springs, where friends wait. They'll set up a lounge chair for him around their swimming pool, put up the burgers on the outdoor grill. Unlike me, he *is* making a giant leap.

When I left, Rick and I had said a sad good-bye. Twenty-seven years of Brooklyn friendship and a certain kind of safety had reached an unexpected depth that poured from my eyes. With Rick on the eighth floor, me on the ninth, it seemed as if we'd shared a duplex. Rick is gay, and our seeming "co-habitation" was uncomplicated. We were aware of each other's movements, the tap running, my footsteps on his ceiling—his singing in the shower drifted through a space in the pipes. We could tell when there were four footsteps, instead of two, and hence knew when we'd have intense relationship conversations in the elevator.

Although Rick wasn't born in Brooklyn, the borough seeped into his blood in the way Brooklyn does. There's that homey, yet upscale paradox—you stand on line to get into an Italian restaurant in Boerum

Hill—yet nothing with red sauce appears on the menu. You walk up Court Street and slip into an unimaginable number of pizza places, with slices sold through storefront windows.

This afternoon Rick and I are meeting at Fortune House on Henry Street; it's my favorite Chinese restaurant because it's so Brooklyn. When people ask me to explain that, I'm at a loss; Brooklyn is a feeling and a nostalgia: Cokes sipped through straws at Packman's Candy Store on Schenectady Avenue, the Top 100 chart at Municipal Records on Eastern Parkway, Murray the K's Rock 'n' Roll shows at The Fox Theater on Fulton Street, kids scattered on every Crown Heights street corner for Kick the Can.

Hipsters take note—I had Brooklyn first!

Today, Rick will tantalize me with details of his new life waiting to be lived. A car with the top down. A condominium twice the size of his co-op, for half the price. New lives are exciting, so filled with hope of what they'll contain, who we'll meet, and mostly who we'll become in our new place.

One of my proudest achievements was leaving Brooklyn. Living where my parents had settled meant never stepping into my own shoes; staying symbolized my inability to live my own life. Still, Brooklyn is in my marrow.

Now I'm settled into my 212 area code and its accompanying blaze of activity. But today, I will return to a quieter place and say another good-bye to Brooklyn.

JOURNEYING

The leap from the edge of Brooklyn to where I landed—fourteen floors above East 42nd Street—felt dramatic. The building's lobby was cavernous with a concierge desk taking up the length of a ten-foot wall. The 325-square-foot studio was charming; walls had molding along the ceiling, as had my Brooklyn place, and a small alcove for my new daybed. The only blemish was the industrial wall-to-wall carpeting.

My windows faced the Ford Foundation; its indoor arboretum reflected upward. On sunny days, the building shimmered. In the distance was the Queensboro Bridge. Headlights beamed back and forth, in movement, everyone going somewhere.

The first several months I sat at my desk, the swivel chair turned sideways toward the windows and took in the expanse. From high above the sidewalk, the sky seemed accessible, inviting. My eyes traced its perimeter, the way the smoggy blue framed skyscrapers and then traveled downtown, uptown, across town. Sometimes my mother's golden-blonde aura seemed to appear, nod approval, maybe in relief that I'd gone in search of my own life.

I breathed a lot, deep belly breaths that nudged me to keep moving, exploring. I was subletting as opposed to renting; that afforded me a feeling of freedom. It felt symbolic that Innovation Luggage was on my corner. Suitcases in every size and color waited to be wheeled out the front door, packed, and slid into overhead. One of the first items I bought was a forest-green Samsonite at T.J. Maxx for sixty dollars. What joy! The bargain, the suitcase on wheels. I had so wanted to be one of those women at airports, trim and confident, maneuvering my baggage as if it weighed two pounds.

Three months later, I packed my carry-on and went to a writers' conference at the University of Iowa. I walked across the sprawling campus and sat by the Iowa River with a notebook; I recalled myself at the Cape Cod writers' conference, the words I had written: *at some point I must be in motion.* Graduates from the university's famed writing program seemed illuminated. I wondered, *What would it be like to go to school here?*

Over the next several months, I burrowed into my Manhattan life. I joined the YMCA, where I took yoga classes; I found a three-day-a-week proofreading job that was a writer's dream—it was stable and paid decently; I met George, whom I dated for a year. He lived around the corner from me. Like my job, he was stable and decent. And I worried about my father, who was determined to live on his own, rather than in assisted living.

I visited him in Florida; we went to his hearing specialist, his internist, his favorite supermarket, Publix. At home, we noshed on roast chicken, played gin rummy, sat by the swimming pool, took taxis to the Chinese buffet. If my father was sad, I hobbled around with his cane to make him laugh.

⟵⟶

I n Manhattan everything was new, alive. A walk to the ATM on 42nd Street meant passing Ann Taylor Loft, the Gap, Cipriani's café. The city glowed. I smiled all the time. I had worked in Manhattan since I was eighteen. Since my thirties and forties, I'd spent many weekends running all over to Chinatown, the Lower East Side, Soho, and every place on the Upper West Side—still, I was naïve, a country girl.

"I just moved out of Brooklyn!" I shared with whomever was near. "I lived there my whole life. Until now, that is." I found excitement in the most mundane places. Bus stops. Coffee shops. In fact, none of my friends who had lived in Manhattan for years knew (as I did) that there was a hardware store on East 29th open twenty-four hours. I walked there at 9:00 p.m. to buy a dish drainer, 11:00 p.m. for potting soil. "You're open all night?" I asked each time, incredulous. This new Manhattan. It was fantastic.

I t *was* fantastic. And yet, something inside of me felt undone. I *was* naïve, younger than my peers in the most basic ways. I didn't think of George as someone to settle down with. *It's not serious,* I said (in the way I had with many men before him). *He's good for now.* In fact, he'd come to me for the short-term. He'd been separated for seven years, but there was no talk of divorce. My studio, with its scant furnishings, had a college-girl feel to it. All I knew about finances came from the book *Investing for Dummies.*

I wasn't ready to settle in. After I'd sold my co-op, paid the broker's fee, credit card debt, a loan from a friend, and three months advance rent plus security deposit, I still had available cash. I *finally* had available cash. I needed to dip into it to pay my Manhattan rent. If I did that long-term, my money wouldn't last long.

I recalled often that wonderful feeling I'd had on the University of Iowa campus. I had the money to pay for school. I researched MFA programs in creative writing. I sent out graduate school applications. They landed in Iowa City, Tucson, Albuquerque, Pittsburgh, Missoula, and Manhattan. Being a fifty-five-year-old graduate student hadn't been my plan when I left Brooklyn. But it became my plan, by default.

Some people call moving through life without a plan "acting on faith." I moved without a plan because of bona fide fear—fear that I would live out my whole life within the landscape of that twenty-seven-year apartment. I must have been really scared, because I don't move easily about the world. In fact, when the acceptance letters came in (and everyone but Missoula said yes), I chose the graduate program built on Manhattan concrete.

My wish to stay still, to become one with life as it happens about and through me, crisscrosses my desire to fly into that expanse of sky, so evident and immaculate, out my window.

Pushed and Pulled

I fell in love with the parks above 42nd Street, in the neighborhood where I lived, called Tudor City. There were classical music concerts on Wednesday evenings, flower plantings that residents were invited to, and benches where people sat and actually talked to one another. And yet, the weeks before I started my MFA program, I was haunted by fantasies of what my life would be like, had I gone to Iowa City Tucson Albuquerque Pittsburgh and sometimes Missoula (even though they said no). My friend Emily, who'd joined me in the application process, did say yes to Iowa. And her yes was rewarded with an Iowa Arts Fellowship. I envied her, not just the fellowship but her ability to embrace the unknown.

Unfortunately, I had remained on Iowa's email list, long after I'd turned their offer down. When I clicked into my email program I was seduced by the correspondence.

Hey all, Want to go to the quarry and hang out?

Does anyone know of an apartment or want to share a house?

Sure! Yeah. Later.

I was fifty-five and wanted to run down to the quarry, share a house, attend classes taught by literary legends. And the reason I wasn't there—I was terrified of the word yes.

Tudor City had its own hundred-square-foot post office, reminding me of Brooklyn Heights. So close to the traffic and stores and throngs of people, and yet away, as if above it all. I often stood on the small bridge known as Tudor City Place, drinking a cup of coffee while looking across the East River toward Long Island City. Then I turned, gazed out over 42nd Street all the way to Times Square. *I live here*, I'd say to myself. *It's unbelievable.*

Yet that other life—or lives, as time went on—pulled at me. There was Tucson, where I imagined I lived in the foothills of the Tucson Mountains, and there was Albuquerque, just an hour-and-a-half drive from Santa Fe, with its own majestic mountains. And I'd read Pittsburgh had been revitalized; the city was thriving.

I prayed that my MFA program, with its own famous faculty, would push me to complete one of the three versions of my memoir. I also prayed it would be so intellectually fulfilling that Iowa Tucson Albuquerque Pittsburgh fantasies would go away.

The first night of classes my professor, Francine, was in the hallway outside the classroom. She held a bouquet of flowers and beamed. A long, fringed shawl draped her small frame. Faculty congratulated her for her inaugural program.

Seven other students were there. I soon discovered Francine had recruited two when she'd met them at an event and interested them in writing a memoir. Two were former students; one was the colleague of a friend. Each was an avid audience. And that was good, because Francine had a lot to say—about herself, the books she'd written, her parents, her heritage. In the two-hour "classes" on writing and craft, perhaps one half of each was on the matter at hand—writing.

All I could think about was Iowa: a classroom jammed with fifteen students, talking narrative arc, point of view, character development. When Francine referred to us as baby writers, a wave turned over in my stomach.

In a private conversation with her, I stammered, "I'm very excited about getting my MFA. But, I'm concerned that the class is for beginners. I've been writing for several years."

I don't recall what she replied. I do recall it wasn't kind.

"I feel infantilized . . ." I stammered.

"I'm sorry I accepted you!" she responded in a tone and a haste that I will never forget.

A conversation ensued. She backtracked and apologized. She said I was scared. We agreed memoir was tricky business; we agreed all my nerves were exposed and that was why I wanted to run. I was lying. But I needed for my decision to stay in New York to be okay. I silently promised that I would never do this again, whatever it was I had done.

My childhood friend, Rochelle, had been a student of philosophy for at least thirty years. I turned to her during that time with my unhappiness.

"I would have stayed in New York, too," Rochelle said, reminding me that she'd never left Brooklyn. We were walking down 42nd Street, past the library on Fifth Avenue. "Look where you live," she said.

I nodded, not impressed.

"I do what's least complicated," Rochelle said. "Moving . . . that would have been very complicated."

"But I'm not happy. I gave up those great opportunities. Yet I can't quit—why?" I kneaded my palm into the right side of my head, something I would do often that year.

"You don't know why you can't. You're not in control of everything, Sandy," she said in her knowing way about the mysteries of the world. "You don't know why you have to be here. Trust that you do."

I breathed deeply. So that was it. My decision to stay was born from the cosmos, not my mixed-up brain. Good to know.

FILLING IN GAPS

From 1996 to 2004, I occasionally received feature article assignments. I had a steady gig for *Complete Woman* magazine, writing self-help articles on relationships. They were all based on some aspect of my own dating life, written in the third person. The way to spin a living out of such work was to refocus the same articles and submit to other publications. I couldn't get the knack of that. Had I been able to earn a living as a freelance writer, it's unlikely that I would have gone to graduate school.

I had thought I was on my way as a freelancer when I landed a few assignments for the *New York Times*. My joy was for the prestige, and it was a way to prove that I had more going for me then an unpublished novel and three unfinished memoirs. But I wrote slowly and over-researched. For two articles I wrote for the "Escapes" section, I spent long hours transcribing notes that strayed far off topic. I put in over a hundred hours on each article; by the time the pieces were accepted, I had earned five dollars an hour for excruciating work.

Freelancing also required having a steel backbone. Rejection was common—for me, that was not the worst of it. I lacked the confidence to call any editor anytime and sell ideas in the one minute he or she gave me.

My mother had often encouraged me to earn a teaching degree. She thought that I would work in the public school system and have summers off like so many people we knew. But teaching at the grade school (or even high school) level never appealed to me. I'd heard too many stories of unhappy teachers who couldn't leave, because of those seductive summers off.

Real gratification through my work life came when I taught my first creative writing workshop. It was for three hours one Saturday morning. That led me to steady part-time work teaching essay writing in continuing education. I began to fantasize a career as a college professor. But I didn't think I could make that life happen.

My mother had attended school through the fifth grade, my father through the eighth, plus Hebrew classes. As adults in America, they wrote phonetically: *Ve luv yu wery much.* In 1959, my parents opened a jewelry store. They used a cash drawer instead of a register. My brother prepared a sheet they kept nearby, with the spelling of numbers from one to ninety-nine, and the words "hundred" and "thousand." I sat with my father once a month as he went through his invoices, and I wrote the checks. I never wondered how he felt about needing me in that way. I never thought he wasn't smart. He read six-hundred-page tomes in English; he loved history, especially books about World War II.

The only two books (I know of) that my mother read, cover to cover, were Grace Metalious's *Peyton Place,* a novel about small-town scandal, and Louise Hay's self-help book *You Can Heal Your Life.* When my parents lived in Florida, my mother sat on a beach chair at the edge of the sand, her skin glistening with Bain De Soleil; she read Hay's book and talked to passersby about how she was healing her life.

I don't know if my mother succeeded; for too many years she had viewed my brother and me as her tonic—that was common for Holocaust survivors. When Lenny and I didn't come through with spouses and grandchildren, my mother was deeply unhappy with her life. By the time she found Louise Hay, her heart had already begun to fail.

STICKING IT OUT

During my second semester of graduate school, we spent an extraordinary amount of class time discussing trauma, abuse, abandonment, any and all suffering for childhoods lost. My family history had provided me much to contribute. But the assigned research articles on trauma were depressing. I longed for Iowa, where I imagined taking a class in "the lyric essay." I became deeply connected to my laptop. I brought it to cafés, where the company of strangers lifted me so that I had distance from the murky past. I wrote; I pushed through.

My third and fourth semesters I had a mentor, Sara. She was the first professor in my program that I genuinely liked. We had lively discussions about moving—although she had traveled from Pakistan, and I (embarrassingly) only from Brooklyn. But, Sara thought my move was huge, that it had a bigger story than I realized. She enjoyed discussing my developing work.

I also took a class on postmodern poets. The professor was talented and loved his job. I claimed my poet's soul. I fell in love with Robert Hayden and Seamus Heaney—two poets who took readers deep below the surface of their words, of their own selves.

To graduate, I amassed a ninety-five-page thesis out of the three hundred or so pages I'd written. I hired an editor to help with organization. I was happy with my thesis, *Halfway Home*, even though it wasn't close to being a book. That was an issue I hadn't foreseen—just how different a thesis can be from a publishable manuscript.

My time in school ended. I was relieved to graduate. Instead of revising *Halfway Home* into a book, I wanted to wrap up the past, send it off to Address Unknown and begin something fresh. And so, I made bows.

My friend's daughter Jill turned two, and I reached into my bag of creativity—a bag (as opposed to baggage) that contains my love of writing as an addendum to numerous other talents that make up my life. For Jill, I took black velvet fabric from the back of the linen closet, folded here, pouffed there, added feathers, beads, and voilà!—two hours had gone by, while I was wondrously consumed by the present moment. And . . . Jill had a bow. I carried on, making bows in tulle, organza, satin, silk, you name it! My bow mania went on for months.

I forget my myriad creative loves too often, especially when caught up in the business side of writing, or the compare side. As in: someone I know will have a book, or two; someone else (from my MFA program!), an essay in a highly regarded journal. I get envious and forget that I'm a fabulous knitter, I cut my own hair, I bake supremely delicious banana muffins.

I love the days when my creative process takes over and I'm completely in tune with the present moment. Regardless of what my work is—bows, essays, muffins—woven into those moments is my greatest life.

REALITY CHECK

My degree gave me entrée to a college teaching career. Unfortunately, my image of myself as a college professor was vastly idealized. That image never included unpaid office hours, hours of paperwork (also unpaid), students sleeping with their heads on their desks, students addicted to technology, and so many with difficult personal lives that they wrote: *I dream about death. When I look in the mirror and see how fat I am I want to kill myself. My father comes home drunk. I'm homeless.* My image never included the emails I would send to counselors with the names of students in emotional trouble.

My first adjunct position was at a college in New Jersey. I continued to proofread two days a week. Of all the wonders of a college teaching job, the commute was most exciting. Two mornings a week, I left at 7:00 a.m., walked to Penn Station and boarded Amtrak headed for New Jersey. We sped through towns crowded with trees; we passed an occasional lake and mounds of earth rising like tiny mountains.

On my walk to school, I picked up a hazelnut iced coffee, then beamed as I walked across the large, busy campus. Everything was perfect, until I had to teach the thesis statement as part of an essay. My writing program hadn't trained me to teach academic English. The only time we had used the word "thesis" it meant the large work we'd complete to graduate. And so, on Day Two of my teaching job, I was stumped.

Part of the course syllabus was to assign students to teach a lesson. Through in-class sample writings, I found a student who would know what a thesis was. I assigned him a ten-minute presentation: the thesis and where it belongs in the essay. (I then said he did a great job.)

As it turned out, my thesis hurdle was a minor blip on my teaching trajectory. The syllabus required six five-page essays (rough and final draft of each) for twenty-two students. Because I taught two classes, I had to read hundreds of pages every other week. I worked until 3:00 a.m., then on the train before class, never quite knowing exactly what I was looking for except for the infamous thesis. I liked the students, and well . . . I loved the train ride out of Manhattan and that stupendous feeling of being on a campus. But I couldn't manage the enormous amount of work. After two months, I quit.

Needing to make sense of the experience, I began a short story "Unraveling."

An underpaid adjunct was not *a glamour job. But Maria wasn't in it for the glamour. She liked the students. She liked their eager faces and the way they looked to her as if she knew things. And she did know things. She knew how to write an essay, how to write exquisite prose. What she didn't know was how to write an* academic *essay.*

I worked on the story for months. Writing helped me move beyond my disappointment. I went on an interview. I found another job.

I'm now well beyond believing in the grains of wisdom I might impart, and I no longer idealize my job. But I do still wonder what would my teaching life would be like if I'd gone off to Iowa City and all the other places?

CHANGING PLACES

My mother had been my go-to parent whenever I telephoned. If my father answered the phone, we'd talk for a few minutes, my mother in the background asking, "Is it *Símala*? Let me talk to her!"

"Here's Mommy," my father would say, and immediately relinquish the receiver.

After she died, I felt my loss most profoundly when I called my father. *Let me talk to Mommy*, I wanted to say. *How is Mommy?* The person who'd been there my whole life could never come to the phone. The gap was immense. I managed to eke out, "I miss Mommy." And my father replied, "I do, too."

We talked every day, sometimes two or three times. I bought my first cell phone in 2004 just so I could call at any time. When my father wasn't home, I tracked him down at a friend's house where he played poker. That he continued to do so after years of card games was a great comfort to me.

My father's position in my life took on a new intensity; at first, that was less from a need for closeness than a sense of duty. He had a rickety walk from two hip replacements and a heel spur. His deafness was of growing concern, mostly because he had refused hearing aids for too long. When he did get them, they were of little value.

As time went on, I noticed things about him I'd never before seen. I discovered there was an elegance to my father; he said "haberdashery" instead of "clothing store," "chiropodist" (where he went often) instead of "podiatrist."

While working on my MFA thesis I had turned to my father for family history. His sister Molly, who had sponsored my parents when they immigrated to America, had left Europe in 1939. To develop my story, I needed details.

"What did Aunt Molly do when she arrived in Philadelphia?" I asked.

"What did she say?"

"No. What did she do? Her work?"

"Her work! The cousins wanted her to be their maid."

"Their maid!" I echoed.

"Do I know how much they paid her?"

"Daddy, how did she end up in Brooklyn?"

"She took a train."

I cradled the phone to my chest, bit my lip, laughed.

If I wasn't prepared with a notebook, I scribbled my father's words on Post-its: *My father picked Hungarian plums from the trees. They were so juicy. My boss's daughter said to me, "I like you." She was ten years old . . . she asked me, "Kiss me!" I was a man! What could I do? I gave her a little peck.*

I stuffed the notes in drawers, found them when I rummaged around for lip balm, aspirin. Yellow papers with sentences scrawled: *My brother cried for one year when our Bubbe died. My father was in agriculture. He sold barrels of plums to grocers.*

⌒

Fortunately, Florida is very good to its elderly—in particular, Holocaust survivors. Through a Jewish agency, he received free services; a young woman came over one day a week to clean and cook. For a small fee, a social worker came to the apartment one day a week to give bereavement counseling. My father never referred to their talks as therapy.

"Elena is so intelligent," he reported to me on the telephone. "We have beautiful conversations."

Then came the mini-strokes—two, about six months apart. Each time, my father rang his neighbor's bell, confused and disheveled; he said simply, "I'm not right." A few times the smoke alarm went off because he forgot he had left water boiling. My brother and I had grown distant and didn't talk about my father's needs; I was grateful for Elena, who helped with finding an assisted-living facility—which my father agreed he needed. But he wasn't happy.

At ninety-three, he moved to a kosher facility in Miami, an hour drive from his shul and friends. He hated it from the first day; he told me, "I'm fenced in, like in a concentration camp." There were many other closer facilities he could've chosen. But there were very few strictly kosher places in Fort Lauderdale and Miami that were also high quality, with independent, healthy residents.

My father's unhappiness at his facility—where he had his own L-shaped studio and where a friendly population lived—consumed me. I Googled "Assisted Living Kosher Florida."

THE WAVY LINE OF CHOICE

I cobbled together a living by teaching four to five courses at two (and sometimes three) colleges. I became an adjunct lecturer at a college that is part of the City University of New York (CUNY) and at a for-profit business college. No mountains, no lakes, just the hard cement I walk on to get to work; I appreciate my walker's commute, the exercise I get, the familiarity; but I also look over my shoulder at the schools and cities where I'm not teaching. I continue to live in a place of "what ifs."

In real time, all four of the English classes I teach are reading Tim O'Brien's *The Things They Carried*. This book about loss and courage, cowardice and survival brings my students to the Vietnam war—a time they know so little of. I tell them about peace marches and draft dodgers, the American flag cut up and sewn to the backs of jackets and worn as bandanas. They smile an embarrassed smile—one that says, *That was a hundred years ago.*

I tell students about young men going to Vietnam carrying the burdens of their country's ambivalence. I tell them what happened after—soldiers returned to a country that had finally moved to one side, the side that disrespected and demeaned those soldiers.

In the chapter "On the Rainy River," O'Brien details the dilemma his main character (who is also called Tim O'Brien) faces upon receiving his draft notice. He wants to be courageous and leave for Canada—but he can't face the disappointment of his community, and so he goes to Vietnam; he considers this an act of cowardice.

The choices we make one day can feel so right, but on another day, so wrong.

When I look back at my important life choices—

getting divorced

remaining single

not having children

living in Brooklyn for so long

saying no to the book packager

not visiting my mother often enough when she was sick

saying no to Iowa City Tucson Albuquerque Pittsburgh

—I wonder, was I a coward to reject situations that were problematic or felt difficult? It's courageous to fight through challenges and anxieties. Would leaving Brooklyn back in 1977 have enabled me to say yes, forever after? Would marriage and children have brought me a lasting peace? If I'd said yes to the book packager, would Brooklyn have been a mere dot on the compass of my life?

Tim O'Brien made the best choice he could at the time; he was on a fishing boat at the border of the United States and Canada. He could have easily freed himself; but his upbringing and all that had taken him to his point of choice led him to turn back, to go to Vietnam. My upbringing and all that led me to points of choice, did not prepare me to fight for what I wanted—or to trust myself to know what I wanted.

O'Brien survived. He wrote a book about those years that I teach almost every semester for its gorgeous prose and brutal insights into the effects of war. And I keep starting memoirs with my own insights into the war my parents lived and how their losses and trauma shaped us.

In a way, O'Brien and I are kindred spirits, fighting wars long over that we can't stop writing about.

A Room of My Own

I 've lived alone for most of my adult life, yet I still luxuriate in a room of my own. Space to myself, where I can prop the laptop on my thighs, listen (or not) to music or the TV's murmur—away from life's tremors—fills me with deep pleasure.

My bookcases rest atop one another and form my bed's headboard. When I read in bed, my pillows prop against the knotty pine wood. Without much twisting I can reach on top for my cup of chai, settle back, nod at the Queensboro Bridge.

I'm lulled by the view out my window and the one behind me. My bookshelves are filled with books by writers who shaped and informed me with their words, helped me to enlarge my identity from a daughter of an Auschwitz survivor to a woman with a wider personality. Nancy Friday's *My Mother/My Self* about mothers' and daughters' separation anxiety echoed my fears of leaving my mother to have my own life. In Erica Jong's *Fear of Flying* I found a character to identify with, one whose dilemma of whether to get a divorce or have a baby was a conflict I'd had when I was married. Frederick Exley, James Kirkwood—male writers I'd found somewhere along the way in my intellectual development. Each writer—male, female—my mentor. My role model. Here I sit, held up by all this knowledge and strength.

I remember when I was a young girl asking my father why there was sadness in the world. And he told me, "In order to know happiness, we must know sorrow." Those were words that defined him, for my father knew deep pain, but when he was happy—when he and my mother danced the *chardash*, a Hungarian folk dance, or when he had a nosh of rye bread with prune butter—he was radiant, fully embodying his happiness.

And so, I believe, my joy with having my own space—my wondrous bounty—is informed by the heartbreak of once losing it.

A day when I was just shy of fourteen, my mother and I apartment hunted in Flatlands, a pretty neighborhood with private homes and lawns, unlike the cement and tar of Crown Heights where we lived. We found an affordable apartment with two bedrooms and an outdoor patio. My mother so wanted that apartment. But moving there meant someone in our family would relinquish a room of his or her own. It wouldn't be my brother, for he was a rebellious teenager, big and messy; he needed a place away from my mother's gaze.

My mother wore her kerchief; her eyes were pools of lost wishes. I could never deny my mother. And so, when she asked, "Can we take this apartment, *mámala*?" I said, "Yes, it's okay," even though everything inside of me shut down.

We packed up the old apartment; at the new one my parents and Lenny filled their new rooms with all they were, and we shopped at Castro for my convertible sofa. We chose an avocado-green loveseat that concealed my twin bed. My desk was in my parents' bedroom, and I shared my mother's closet. My sweaters and underwear were in a bureau in my brother's room. My private spaces were the bathroom and the pantry (where I talked on the telephone).

Today, whenever I see a teenage girl's room cluttered with all she might become, a pang of regret fills me. I want to go back so many years ago and tell my mother, "No. It's not okay." And that's not because I'd get a room; it's to give my voice expression.

Sometimes I wonder if I haven't remarried because I'm afraid of losing my space, and therefore, myself. For space defines me. Having it makes me one person. Not having it makes me another. If I lived with someone, could we co-exist in this one room? Would it make a difference if we had a mansion?

It's rare that I take for granted this studio apartment above the city, so far removed from that Castro sofa bed and all it denied.

A Teacher's Dignity

I'm seated in front of my remedial writing class with a tower of papers on the edge of my desk. A student a few feet in front of me says, "I'd rather wash floors than have your job." At moments like this, I tell my students my academic history and just how deep the comment hits.

I was ashamed that I didn't have the academics to be a liberal arts student, a real college girl, like my adolescent literary heroines, twins Pam and Penny. Author Rosamond du Jardin's Double Date books about the sisters shaped my dreams; but my upbringing shaped my real-life student experiences.

At my community college, there was no sorority, no campus, no anxiety over my typing and steno courses in my secretarial program. I didn't take math, science, or a foreign language. Seven years out, with my Associate in Applied Science (AAS) degree framed and shelved, I applied to Hunter College, a real college. I was accepted, and not surprisingly, was placed in remedial math. And one year later, after passing that class and several others, I dropped out because college didn't feel right; three years later I tried again, and graduated from New York University.

In the telling and retelling of my history, it's become like so many other shameful experiences, a story to help others. This is the part that

I want my students to hear—that these fifteen weeks of class that they may cut, sleep through, be embarrassed about, in denial over—will one day be a story. And if they tell it right, a good story!

In my own remedial class, the expectation was that I would learn algebra, geometry, and trigonometry in fifteen weeks. Shame and then fear that I wouldn't pass immediately rose up. I hired a tutor, and between our twice-weekly sessions and my classes, I did learn three years of math in fifteen weeks. My B in that course is to this day the most fulfilling of all the grades I've received—and there have been many. The reason: that was the only course I was sure I wouldn't grasp. I get a great rush from proving my limited beliefs of myself to be wrong.

I took the GREs when I applied to graduate schools. Twenty points is the lowest you can score, 800 the highest. My math score was 40. But I got into some of the best writing programs in the country. And I think that had to do with the story I wrote for my personal statement about my very sad and crooked education.

My students often compare me to another teacher, who has looser rules. I ask them, what is your goal? To never have to take this class again or hang out with friends? They're college students; they want to hang out. Many think they're in the class because their entrance exam essay was graded wrong. I get upset when they seem not to care.

Today was stressful all around. Research papers are coming due, which means annotations, APA, MLA—all that non-creative stuff I hate teaching. There's *Halfway Home* I could start revising into a book (were I inclined to do so). But I'm stressing over students. Why do I care, if many of them don't?

I think it comes back to what my student said; once I take the dignity out of my job—and that's all about caring—I am washing floors.

STOLEN TIME

Downward-facing dog and spinal twists feel good in my body. I linger in each pose, long after the teacher has moved on. My upper torso reaches one way, my legs another. In spinal twist, being in two places at the same time is possible, preferred. Maybe that's why my mind drifts, seeks a *drishti*, a point of focus.

But I never drift away at 4:00 a.m. Four o'clock in the morning is my luscious Manhattan time. I awake; instead of willing myself back to sleep, I say hello to the day. I have a mug of steaming hazelnut coffee on my date with the sleepy world. To me, this is the height of decadence, coffee at 4:00 a.m.

I gaze out into the dark and smile at my date; I'm so grateful, it's just us.

My beau George loved theater and opera. He would have taken me every night if I'd wanted. But his New York City didn't excite me as much as my twenty-four-hour-hardware-store New York City.

⌒

In the early morning hours, I turn on the computer and look for assisted-living facilities. My father's unhappiness leaks into my dreams. Special Transportation Service (STS) can take him anywhere (within reason) he wants to go, but requires paperwork from his doctor, who is in Fort Lauderdale. My father gave his doctor the forms when a friend drove him to the office; his doctor says he faxed the papers. STS doesn't have them. The facility steps in and says we have to start from the beginning.

When I visit, we *could* take a taxi back and forth to his doctor; I *could* rent a car, although I haven't driven in twenty years. We *could* find options. But instead, we sit, like two old souls, in plastic armchairs in front of the facility. We munch on peanuts and pretzels, gaze at the twisty tree trunks that are aged and graceful. We seal one another in life and in memory.

W hen not trying to help my father, I narcissistically type my name into Google. I do this to verify my existence in the world. When, voilà!, my name appears, I see me, from the outside. (Articles and essays I wrote, plus student reviews on Rate My Professors—my favorite comment: *She's so sweet and extremely understanding. That being said, though, you shouldn't take advantage of her, because she will remember.*) When I find me on the Internet, I'm confirmed as a person with more than a thought bubble around her head. These little bits of information mirror to me that I'm in the world and working, writing, living.

If it's a workday, I get lost in agendas to ease my anxiety. Have I prepared enough to fill a seventy-five-minute class or an hour-and-forty-five-minute class (at the business college)? An essay for us to read and dissect—sixty minutes at least. Annie Dillard's "The Chase" is especially good for time consumption.

Dillard's story of her girlhood in Pittsburgh when she was seven years old and had "an arm like a boy" is filled with metaphors and grammar choices: semicolons, dashes, parentheses. I tell my students, "Think of parentheses as a whisper; use dashes to emphasize. What about the semicolon; why did she use that instead of a period? Remember, there are rules, but you also have choices."

Then there's fifteen minutes for free writes: five minutes of timed writing, then five minutes jumping off the first timed writing, then five minutes to underline favorite sentences, phrases that have good energy. Something to start with when they do the at-home assignment: write about an event from your childhood—a race, a game, a move, something memorable—and draw the story out for two pages.

Once a student wrote about a sexual encounter. His paper, specific and vulgar, held not one lyrical word. I returned it to him and told him use Dillard's essay as a model. *She was seven years old.*

Now I tell students, "Keep it clean." There are teachers who disagree with my limits; but I don't want my class to devolve into embarrassed laughter and much worse. We're not a creative writing class. It's English Composition 101. There is so much to teach them beyond what they already know.

What to Write

I began an anonymous blog to test my ability to write LIVE and see if I had the writing stamina to keep a blog going. I loved to dance, and so I called myself "Isadora" for the dancer Isadora Duncan. She was a free spirit who eschewed the norms of her time (as I felt I did—or wanted to do).

Through my blog I enjoyed the freedom of writing openly about my life as a single woman having a relationship with Manhattan. Would it be a fling or something more serious? I didn't know that my blog's theme would change dramatically.

A telephone call came at 4:00 p.m. When I saw the 305 area code that wasn't my father's number, I braced myself. It was the receptionist at his assisted-living facility; he'd had a stroke. I packed, grabbed my laptop, then a taxi and flew to my father, whom I'd spoken to earlier that day to wish him a happy Father's Day. Even with an amplified phone device, he could barely hear me. There was a lot of static, too; I don't know if he knew it was me.

In the hospital when I arrived, my father wasn't able to speak; but his eyes widened and smiled with relief. There were so many doctors and nurses; they marveled at his energy (he tried several times to get out of bed) and his alertness.

My father and I communicated through kissing each other's hands. "Can you hear me, Daddy?" I asked, and he lifted my hand to his lips. I took his hand to mine. Most often I simply asked, "Kiss me, Daddy," and he kissed my hand.

I went back and forth from my father's apartment to the hospital. I felt safe in the assisted-living facility. His neighbors asked, "How is Bernie?" They invited me to dinner. No matter where I went, I carried my laptop and blogged like crazy. Knowing my friends read every word got me through. Especially when a doctor asked if my father had a DNR (Do Not Resuscitate). I leaned against the wall and sobbed. But then, later that day my father's situation was determined hopeful enough for him to enter a rehab facility.

The following morning my father was aware of me and a speech therapist. She told me I talked to him too fast, was too animated. She gave me a pamphlet with instructions. I was irritable, suddenly angry at my father. *You weren't such a good father* flashed through my mind. I recalled arguments he'd had with my mother when I'd sat between them, my head turning this way and that like at a tennis match. And when my father had discovered my relationship years before with a Catholic man, he'd threatened to disown me.

The Miami sun beamed through the window. I wanted to go outside, bathe in the light. And so I left the hospital before I said something regrettable. If my father knew I was about to explore a city I didn't know, he'd have begged me not to go.

Walking though the hospital parking lot, I felt surreal—free in a horribly forbidden way. I asked directions, walked a few blocks south, then made a right west. I found downtown Miami. It was blistering hot. I called my friend Stephanie.

"My father started rehab. He's going into a facility. I'm packing a small bag for him tonight—gym shorts, sneakers, polo shirts."

"Rehab! That's good, Sandy. That's hopeful."

"Yes . . . I'm relieved."

"How long will you stay there?"

"I don't know. I want to go home. I miss home."

I settled in at Dunkin' Donuts to set up my computer. My blog was a living, breathing thing.

A few hours later, I went back to my father's apartment. I noticed his watch on the kitchen table; it was odd that he'd taken it off. My father was once a watchmaker. He always wore the silver chain-link timepiece. I put it on. I also put on his gold *chai*, which he'd designed in the shape of a rooster. The quirky Jewish symbol dangled on a heavy chain.

I went to sleep early—on the couch, as I did every night I was there; I couldn't sleep in my father's bed. The phone rang around 2:00 a.m. I calmly answered, as if I'd been waiting for it. "Your father passed away," the distant voice said. I dressed and grabbed my laptop, held it close.

In the hospital, I called my brother; our distance rendered us unable to offer solace to each other. Then I mechanically made the required phone calls. If not for my laptop, I would have been alone. I opened my graduation thesis and cut a section I'd written when my father was alive. I pasted it into my blog:

My father's heart has six cracked edges I run my fingers over when I put my hand against his chest. Each edge has a name

Leibich.

Miriam.

Wolf.

David.

Herschel.

Mendel.

My father's parents and four brothers. Killed in ovens big enough to hold people. Now they are inscribed in the book of life.

Then I added: *Tonight, my gorgeous father, Bernard, passed away. His Czech name was Bela. Now my father, Bela, is with his family.*

I wrote to the degree I could allow myself, careful to not bleed on my readers.

I needed them to return to my pages, to help me manage my grief. I came home to New York two days later.

Saying Yes

O n my third day of sitting shiva, I received an email from Poetica
Publishing, a small literary press, in response to my query of a
few months before. They said yes to co-publishing my essay collection,
On My Way to Someplace Else. This work was a compilation of essays
I had published individually. When I read the email, I felt strange. A
happy feeling cracked through my grief, like happiness that cried.

I replied: *Yes Yes Yes.* For one of the few times in my life, I asked no
one for advice. I signed an agreement, and that was that. I didn't know
that "co-publishing" was an eloquent term for self-publishing; it didn't
matter what it meant. I needed something great to happen in those early days after my father died, and there it was—my book.

My father would have loved to share in the process, and I so loved
feeling his pride. But he would have had trouble with the one essay I
wrote about him, "The People we Love and Create," which went like
this:

*My father's hold on me is silent. It is in the curve of his shoulders, the
slope of his eyes, the smile that asks for permission.*

*"Símala," he says into my answering machine, "it's Daddy." I hear
his voice and I become eight years old, the age at which he still believed
I would remain forever like a wind-up doll—smiling, child-like, obedient.*

I disappointed him gravely. I haven't been inside a synagogue in years, date only Christian men, and have renounced marriage and motherhood altogether.

When I was a young, single woman, struggling for independence, I pushed away his palms filled with cash, the shopping bags he brought to my door filled with lamb chops and steaks from the kosher butcher. When I watched him from my window, placing the bundles back into his car, my heart broke.

One day while I was moving furniture around my apartment, the channel changer broke off my television. Not wanting to purchase a new TV, I discovered that I could use pliers to change channels. Every day my father called, and in a voice thick with anxiety, he asked, "You're still using the pliers?" to which I responded, "I'm fine Dad, how are you?"

The pliers became a bitter tango between the two of us, until I came home one day and found him standing outside my apartment building, next to a large carton, marked Magnavox. As we rode up in the elevator, the box between us, the sweet flicker of independence I knew only in spurts, gave way and I saw the father of my childhood, a man with nothing to live for but the opportunity to fix his daughter's life.

After my mother died, my father and I made peace with who the other was. We didn't have the luxury of nursing old hurts. We needed each other—I used to think my father more so, but I needed to love someone wholly.

QUESTIONING

I checked in with the website www.shewrites.com, where women writers post comments about their projects. One writer working on a Holocaust memoir said she's concerned that people no longer want to read about that subject.

Since the mid-1990s—when the fiftieth anniversary of the Jews' liberation was celebrated—there have been many memoirs by survivors and their families. About ten years ago, a book review in the *New York Times* said the topic is overdone. Does that mean the Holocaust and all its ramifications are passé?

In the weeks since my father's passing, I'm being revised. My insights and understanding of him change so swiftly, I can't keep up. His mail is forwarded to me: Medicare, telephone, doctors, banking. So much paperwork occupied my father's daily life. *How many hours did he spend making phone calls?* A horrible image of him being put on hold then transferred to voice mail, then back and forth, fills me with sadness.

I imagine my father before the war and after. The ninety-four-year-old man I walked hand in hand with, on the lawn of his assisted-living facility, morphs into the stunning young man he was, wearing a dark suit and tie, starched white shirt, when he stood next to my mother in her borrowed bridal gown at their wedding. The father he could have been before the Holocaust would have been quite different than the one he became.

My father's loyalty and devotion were always part of him. The war did not take those qualities away, but did intensify them. When I moved into that Brooklyn Heights apartment as a divorced woman, the moment my father heard the hint of need in my voice, he'd gasp, "What's wrong?" I'd say, "Why do you always think that?" Thirty minutes later my doorbell would ring; there he'd stand, his shoulders hunched, weighed down by bottles of Diet 7-Up, twenty cans of tuna fish, and everything else he carried.

Like all children of survivors, I was handed a task at my birth: to understand and love the person my father was before while interacting with the parent who bore the aftereffects.

On this sunny Sunday morning, the Holocaust is alive. It breathes and sighs upon me.

The New Book

Before my essay collection went into production, I farmed out portions to writer friends, asking for last-minute comments on my essays. They came through with just the right insights and fixes. I have amazing people around me. (I must remember that.) Then I made one last tiny change, hit "send" and off the corrected manuscript went to the editor.

My peace lasted three seconds; I suddenly detested my last (did I mention, tiny?) change, which felt enormous—in fact, I felt *ruined* the entire tone. An hour later, the editor, Michal, emailed, *I can't open your attachment. Please resend.* Sometimes, not just people but every bit of life is amazing.

I undid the change and sent the collection the next day from my more-dependable office computer.

I received a back-cover blurb today (now I have three) that made my eyes tear. It spoke of me as a daughter of survivors, the horrible conflict of parent and child. The reviewer completely understood the work, and thus, me.

I had a fantasy of reading from my book at my father's assisted-living home, with him there and alive. I choose an excerpt from an essay.

I see my father forty years ago, leaning into the Yiddish newspaper, weakness etched into his silhouette, and I wonder, was it his fragility I saw, or my own inability to turn back time, to undo the works of Hitler? I love my father perhaps more than I love myself. He smiles, and I go weak.

After I read, my father and I make the rounds of Miami synagogues, and he's seated in the front row. There I am on a panel discussing important issues Jewish writers discuss. Beneath all the hoopla, what I'm really doing is imagining an ending to my father's life, when I make up for all his losses.

I wonder, if I'd had children, would I have handed the baton to them? Would my happiness be their responsibility? In my wildest dreams of myself as a mother, I raise children who are risk takers, "yes" people.

What I Need as a Writer

At a panel discussion for writers I once attended, participants who had published books were asked to stand and take a bow. My self-published collection wasn't yet out in the world—and some might argue, *self*-published wasn't what was meant. But I stood anyway. And while standing I recalled the book packager from so many years before. Had I said yes to him, I imagined I'd be standing quite proudly, that is if I wasn't busy counting all my money.

During that week, I wrestled with myself over what kind of writer I was—book or essayist. My first essay, "A Daughter's Legacy," about my relationship with my parents, was delivered in fifteen hundred words. My next work was about my relationship to dieting, in twelve hundred words. Then "Keeping Alive the Dreams of Love" (twelve hundred and fifty words) came out in the *Times,* and soon after I started my novel *Knitting Lessons.* Although I loved the process of inventing characters, at heart, I was more comfortable with things that really happened. And writing in the short form served me.

But I have had my dreams of stunning Oprah moments, heard her call my book-length memoir compelling, gorgeous, triumphant! But my love for the labor of writing essays has trumped my need for flashy success. I get derailed, though, when I see the books my peers are writing and publishing.

When I read of their contracts.

When I log onto a website and all I see is book book book.

In neon.

And when I get lost in envy, I beat myself for lagging behind.

Self-publishing *On My Way to Someplace Else* was partially born from a desire to make it in this book arena. But, more important, I wanted to honor my Holocaust legacy by having a product to contribute to libraries around the world. And not least of all, I needed to honor my writing process by compiling into a collection each precious essay that was written, revised, critiqued, labored over, and that filled my morning hours with complete happiness.

Taking control of the process enabled me to get my work out in the world quickly. Quite likely it was my only way. Agents I had queried said essay collections by unknowns were a tough sell to publishers. Small presses I had contacted said they couldn't market the book, as it wasn't focused on one theme—say, the Holocaust—but was also about dating, walking, knitting, simply living my life.

Now, it is 4:30 a.m. I'm ruminating on my thesis, aka *Halfway Home*. Can I let it go and ignore the fact that I spent years on it? The revision process keeps my parents present and alive, nowhere near that gift-wrapped box I'd envisioned while still in graduate school.

WHERE PEACE RESIDES

Sometimes I talk or email with Emily, the friend who did go off to Iowa. She's different, or *we're* different. She doesn't ask me to read her work as she once did. She recently critiqued an essay I wrote; her comments recommended an overhaul: *delete the first page, develop one really good sentence on page two into the opening paragraph.* Fine comments, all—or at least, I think so. I didn't do any of that, though. Her suggestions, once light-handed, seemed informed by a writing program instead of the writer Emily was before.

Some of her Iowa peers stayed after graduation; they bought houses, found partners, made lives. Each time Emily and I speak, I imagine buying a house in Iowa, meeting a small-town guy (a carpenter!), baking banana muffins for my neighbors. And I also feel awkward—our school choices moved us away from each other. I marvel at her confidence, her ability to move from her home in Chicago to Brooklyn where we met, then Iowa City and now New Hampshire. I want that confidence, or is it something else Emily possesses? Trust in life's random choices, knowledge that it's safe to move about the world? Are most people yes people?

One of my yoga teachers says, "Whatever you feel on the mat, you feel in your life." My landlord, Laura, allowed me to have the dreary wall-to-wall carpeting lifted; the dark wood floor beneath is worn in places but more pleasing to live in. Now when I lay down my mat, the surface is harder, steadier. My palms and the soles of my feet have traction when I'm in downward dog.

Does that mean I don't have to move across the country to find my place, but rather, can make one small but necessary change?

PERSPECTIVE

Yesterday I tried a new yoga studio that had been highly recommended. I was the only one who showed up for the 9:00 a.m. class. It was like winning the lottery. The teacher used our ninety minutes to design a practice for me—two actually, one for morning and one for evening. We talked a lot, too, about how I don't want my practice to be an audition for the Cirque de Soleil. I do want the rewards to filter through my day, to be inside me when I teach and get caught up in students' needs, especially those that have nothing to do with the lesson.

When I came home from class, I rearranged all my furniture. I had an urge to open up my space, especially to move the sofa that divided my studio into two rooms. Peace may be about standing still, taking in the Zen of the situation and being peaceful in two rooms. But it was easier for me to move the couch.

When I look toward the windows, my eyes sweep across the open space. The apartment appears airy and light. Since my father died, my viewpoint shifts. One day I want to feel cocooned, another day to feel I can fly. And so I write at 4:00 a.m., my wondrous hour. And I wonder if I can fly and feel safe at the same time.

TALKING TO MY FATHER

While walking to work today, I had a long talk with my father. It hit me a few blocks from home that I felt disconnected from the pain of losing him. I didn't want the pain in all its force, just a reminder of it these few months later—a lingering sense of grief, a hollowness. How else to pay honor to my father's ninety-four years of life?

And so I conjured him. *Hi Dad!* I said. *How are you?* I was happy, so happy, in that awkward state of knowing the awfulness of losing him and his unbelievable return. *Hiya,* mámala, he said. Two faces came into view my father with steel-white hair (sort of like Zorba the Greek) and the gorgeous man he was at thirty-five, with his high, regal forehead, his shy, apologetic smile. Both images filled my mind's eye. It was so good to see him.

As I walked, I saw myself at my computer, tapping out the story of my father's American life.

When he and my mother arrived in 1947, he was husky, hairy with thick shoulders and arms. At night he worked for a butcher, cleaning the innards of chickens and cows. During the day he worked in a lingerie factory as a cutter, pressing his palms atop the patterns, sealing the paper to the fabric. In 1959, he studied under his brother, Moishe's tutelage, to become a watchmaker. When my parents opened their first jewelry store in the East New York section of Brooklyn, my mother was the heart of the store; she kibitzed with customers, sold charms, bracelets, any item she wore that day. My father stood behind a see-through panel, his jeweler's eye like a thimble on his forehead. He leaned into his work space, soldering guards on rings and giving watches back their tick. My father was the store's quiet, studious soul, bent as if in prayer.

By the time I arrived at work, I had a good old-fashioned heartache.

In *Prozac Diary,* Lauren Slater claims Prozac robbed her of her writing instinct. Mental health came with a price—no tortured material. Illness had given her imaginary friends, obsessions, delusions to fill her pages. She wanted off Prozac.

In the loss of my father, I'm a woman without parents, two people who had an overwhelming need to fill my hands with all they would and wouldn't hold. I'm a woman without the confusion of our intense and conflicted love. There was always something from which I was breaking free. An obstacle high as the moon. My life's journey has been searching for a place—and a way—to have my own life. I'm a woman without a map. And how will I get there without something pulling me back?

CLEANING HOUSE

There's a scene in *Halfway Home* that takes place when I'm a teenager and my mother teaches me how to clean the bathroom. She taught me to ball up damp toilet paper in my hand, and then, on my hands and knees, to wipe the floor repeatedly—especially the corners—until I found no trace of hair.

My mother had a fixation with hair. Her job at Auschwitz was cleaning the latrines, scrubbing the toilets and floors—where I believe her hair madness began. Whenever she found strands in the sink, tub, or floor, something crazy took hold of her. And so, every Saturday I cleaned the bathroom exactly as she wanted. To this day, I'm vigilant when using any bathroom, careful to leave behind not a trace of hair.

The editor who helped me organize the MFA thesis suggested beginning with the scene of my mother and me on our hands and knees. I disagreed, as I didn't see that event as something that had shaped me. It seemed a gratuitous opening hook, a nod to the Holocaust. To me, this scene was very sad, but not material to play with. I wanted instead to open:

I was five, six, seven when I sat curled with my mother in the living room in our apartment in Crown Heights. We sat on the wide, bulky chair

that was also known as "Mommy's chair." It was there my mother kept
her past alive by telling me about her life.

I ended up opening in the present, looking out the window at the
Queensboro Bridge. From there, my words found their way to the wide,
bulky chair.

But this week I remember my editor's advice, for I've been on my
hands and knees cleaning my apartment floor. My work life—with four
classes concurrently writing research papers—is stressful. I'm also
fearful my essay collection will have glaring errors that embarrass me.
There's a nasty little copyedit error in my biography on the back cover:
She's a craftsperson and award-winning writer. The missing "an" before
award-winning makes me squirm; so, too, does the realization that the
full-sized image of my cover I'd approved looks quite different in its
actual size.

I miss my father. I clean. I take to the earth, a damp towel in my
palm, wiping the floor, getting that dirt and hair off. The gratification
is immediate. There is dirt beneath dirt. So much to wipe up, to find on
my towel. Each discarded towel brings relief. I turn up the radio. Dance
a bit.

My father had come to symbolize my mother. When he passed
away, I lost my mother all over again. And this week, stress literally
sending me to my hands and knees, I understand why she honed that
posture. As my editor thought, yes, it was a repetition of an awful pain.
But it was also a way to bring order to a mind in a constant spin. What
peace, to stand finally, and gaze upon a spotless floor. Not one strand of
hair! And when something outside that room went awry, how lovely to
return to the safety of the floor. Kneel. And clean.

WANTING

*O*n *My Way to Someplace Else* will be here in a few weeks. I ordered two hundred books. The book success I didn't think I wanted yet I always knew I did will soon arrive in all its flawed perfection. I hope to spend the rest of my life reaching for everything else I don't want but so very much do.

By writing this about my good news, I am spitting in the face of the evil eye and my mother's lessons about revealing personal information.

My mother was deeply fearful of the evil eye. She was vigilant about not telling people good things about our family. She believed their jealousy would cause them to swoop in and snatch her treasures, the very treasures that had been so hard to accumulate and possess.

When I get a job or anything I desperately want, or publish an essay someplace great, I tell a chosen few, those who I am certain as possible are so happy with their lives, they could never cast an evil glance my way.

My mother had a method for protecting herself when it wasn't possible to withhold good news: she made a fist and slipped her thumb between her index and middle fingers. I can't tell you how many times I've walked the earth with my hand in this knot. When I notice this reflexive response to having spilled good news, I look upward and smile at my mother, aware of her approval.

Lately: I fight the urge to make the special fist.

I fight the urge to live in fear of taking chances.

I fight for the right to have my own beliefs.

EXPECTATIONS

My freshman students expect to receive high grades, and that means As. That also means not all understand what it means to earn an A. A student who is late for every class excuses it as: *But I was printing out* your *assignment.* Cs on three papers: *But I contribute to class more than anyone.* Talks to neighbor during class: *I asked him about the assignment.* I wish they would all get As because I like giving high grades. But what do I make of students with low regard for classroom policies, students who don't take responsibility, and the worst— technology abusers?

I remember passing notes in high school during teachers' lectures. I loved the camaraderie with another student and being mischievous together. If we'd had texting back then, likely I would have been an avid user. But I didn't care about grades in my high school years, which was reflected in my academic record. Raised to be a secretary, I was a low achiever. That wasn't a problem until years later. My high-achieving peers found enviable jobs in fields like advertising and education. It took me years to catch up.

Today, in the confines of the adjunct office, instructors have little time to talk; we're racing to use the coveted school resources like the printer and the copier. But one thing we often weigh in on is cell phone use in class. Whether or not we were once like our students is inconsequential. Especially after standing in front of the classroom for upwards of an hour to three, after spending at-home time preparing, travel time getting in early to read papers, plan some more. As soon as a student starts playing with his or her phone, my younger self, playing with the split ends of my Mary Tyler Moore flip, vanishes from my mind. There is only the moment of realization—perhaps, wrongly—this student doesn't care.

In one class last semester, while a few students made a presentation, I sat with the rest of the class, took out my phone and pretended to text. Then I put my head on the desk miming the worst of my class. Students roared with laughter. But nothing changed.

Some students will always test the limits. I feel sad for them because I know the risks. Falling off track takes seconds; getting back on track takes years. I lived those years painfully, before getting serious and caring.

A BALANCING ACT

I read an advice column this morning in *The Chronicle of Higher Education*, "I Hate Myself When I'm Teaching." I've been feeling the same sentiment a lot lately. The desire to reach (and please) every student rises up in me each time I gaze upon ten to thirty faces. My competition is fierce—electronic devices, the ticking clock, the students' dislike of the assigned reading, and me . . . well, I'll avoid that one for now.

Students who attend commuter schools in large urban cities often have jobs as well. I remember what that was like when I went to college at thirty years old; working, making time for the library, writing papers, and attending class all during the same semester was tough. Teachers often have an equal amount of stress. I teach two sections of the same English composition class, back to back. How much easier my life would be if the classes perfectly aligned—thirty minutes in one class for a lesson on summary versus paraphrase is forty-five minutes in another; an hour to analyze an essay in one class versus the full class in the other. Each class has a distinct personality; one class's engagement with a topic is another class's ho-hum.

But then, there are days I love myself when I'm teaching. A student will say, "I'm actually learning something," or, "This is one class

I'd never cut," or, simply, will stop by just to say hello during my office hours. There's so much about teaching you can only learn by being there. Like how it feels when a student sends an email saying his sibling just died in an accident. Especially when this very student is behind in assignments and you planned to discuss this (firmly) after the next class. There's the student who arrives a half hour late every morning. Then he or she hands in a paper about recovering from the loss of his parent—about surviving. A teacher—this teacher—has to know how to enforce academic standards while pulled by the strains of compassion.

Teaching means tolerating the love/hate relationship I have with my own abilities, trusting it will morph into something kinder.

BEAUTIES, EVERY ONE

I heard that a Miss Holocaust Survivor pageant was held in Israel. The news report on BBC Radio said two sides debated the rightness of such an event. On one side were those who felt the women were used (and denigrated) to market cosmetics. On the other side were those who felt the pageant was a way to celebrate life.

I see both viewpoints; however, for survivors like my mother, who cleaned toilets, and like her sister Shari, who carried corpses to the crematorium, it would take a lot more than pushing cosmetics to feel denigrated.

One of the miracles of my mother's life, and this may sound trivial, is that six months after her liberation, she was stunningly beautiful. She entered Auschwitz a frizzy-haired fifteen-year-old girl, somewhat wild-eyed and untamed. In photographs of her after, she has long, brown hair, grown back so fast and high atop her forehead in a pompadour. Her wide-lipped smile is radiant.

The Miss Holocaust Survivor pageant was an acknowledgment of how important physical beauty was to the women, and to the one I knew best, my mother. In America, after she gave birth to my brother, she piled her thick, brown, wavy hair atop her head and colored her full lips cherry red. Neighbors said she was an Ava Gardner look-alike until she dyed her hair blonde and became a Gabor.

My mother's sister Ahgie, with her wholesome good looks and toothy smile, looked like Dinah Shore, and my father's sister, Sylvia, was a dark-haired beauty likened to Liz Taylor. There was my aunt Frieda (not a survivor but an immigrant), who's bosomy physique was often compared to Mae West; my father, with his rippled brown hair brushed back, resembled Ralph Bellamy; my gorgeous Uncle Bela, who starred in a Vlasic pickle commercial, was a movie star in his own right.

We were primitive people and we created ourselves through the images we found in American culture. My mother's beauty saved her life—certainly her spirit—for when nothing else seemed to exist for her, she found enormous comfort in self-care and grooming. The simplest mood lifter she bequeathed to me was in the healing power of taking care of my body.

Were my mother alive (and in Israel), she would have been a fabulous pageant contender. But I hate to think of how it would feel to her to lose. I can see my father flick his wrist, say, *What's the big deal?* It would have been a very big deal. No one could have possibly been a better Miss Holocaust Survivor than my mother.

Cautiously Happy

My two hundred copies of *On My Way to Someplace Else* really are on their way to someplace else. They didn't arrive. Instead, my computer died. I was certain these events had something to do with my having spit in the face of the evil eye. And so I covered myself in all my mother's voodoo charms, slipped my thumb through my fist. What else could I do? The books arrived Wednesday; my computer came back to life.

I have my books, my computer, and my indelible connection to a long line of ancestors who lived in fear of merciless curses being cast their way.

Not Remembering

I n *Writing Down the Bones*, Natalie Goldberg suggests the writing prompts "I remember" and "I don't remember." When I give this exercise to a class, most students discover that "I don't remember" brings them up close to a memory in greater detail than "I remember." When not trying hard to recall the past, our unconscious material (years and years of it) swims to the surface. This continually happens to me in my grief for my father. New ways of remembering him slice through the memories I had when he was alive, turning them inside out.

When my father was alive, I didn't idealize him. I didn't realize it at the time, but I exaggerated his flaws so that I could separate from him. *He drives me crazy,* I'd say, to validate the arguments I now wish we hadn't had. Now that he's gone—the separation definite—he vividly appears: my perfect father. He's driving his cream-colored, two-door Buick, his elbow resting on the window frame, as he brakes and slows in front of my apartment building.

It's so tempting to bog down in new ways of remembering my father, to idle inside regret. This is my nature. But then, that would taint the grace and purpose of Goldberg's writing prompt. In a real-time, face-to-face encounter, I'm not sure it's possible to not remember in all its truth and rawness. It's only after, when the mind is like putty, that it can look into the underbelly of what was.

WRITING THROUGH IT

I sit at the counter of the Russian-owned Sunburst Espresso Bar on Third Avenue and Eighteenth. The scents of almond scones and strong coffee waft through the air. Heavily accented voices mix with the clatter of coffee cups and spoons. I'm at home here, where Eastern Europe is thickly brewed.

Daylight pores in. I sip my café au lait and enjoy the soft warmth of steamed milk on my upper lip. I open the laptop, lazily scroll through my folders for *Halfway Home*. I land at my thesis and then, my email box goes orange—hooray—a distraction! But when I open the email, I'm not glad at all, for it's not a nice email. It's a friend who is angry at me. He'd called a few days before when I was unable to listen to his problems.

Now his email voice cuts through my day and hits a sensitive chord. The only good thing about it is that I now know what to write about.

Early in my career, I cried when I wrote. I loved every second of it. I remember writing a story about a young boy in Czechoslovakia in 1944. Avram saw his parents and siblings killed by the SS. In spite of his heartache, he fought for his life. He jumped off trucks, ran right when everyone ran left. He survived and made it to America.

I felt as if Avram was my father and that memory and imagination had entwined. I had never cried so hard in my life. When I read the story to my mother, she said that I was Avram. She said that his parents were really my father and she . . . alive but wounded. I was deeply moved to learn my mother understood me at such a level.

I worked on the story obsessively. And I cried a little less each time. Eventually the story became a thing outside me. I sculpted it by editing here, adding stuff there. And then I sent it into the world. This thing that came from deep inside, mottled with tears and rage, took on a value as art—or at least, as a compass, helping me find and release a deep pain.

It's wonderful to cry while writing; laughter is great, too. Anything that takes me into the marrow of the bone—the sensitive place where my friend's email hit. He brought me to a time and place when my parents' need for me to remain close was the center of me. I battled against that into adulthood and then one day my father became elderly, a widower, and needed me even more, although to fight the reality of aging, he tried to need me less. "Don't worry so much," he said, when I couldn't reach him at home and called all his friends. "I can do for myself," he said, when he first had a helper to cook and shop. When I visited, the best I could do was sit at the table, play gin rummy.

Now he's gone, and I grieve for him. Yet I'm also easing into a new life, where I can say no when I must, without guilt. In my story of Avram, he wept for his family, but he saved himself. If my mother was right that I was Avram—and she so often was right—then I must choose my own life. And while doing so, I might not be there for the friend who needs me.

Moving On

My book has the perfect cover: a photograph of my mother and me (at four years old) holding hands. I look up at her face, she down at mine, both of us in a complete state of rapture.

I filled a shopping bag with the books and I hit the pavement. I stopped at independent bookstores and left review copies. I can't recall the last time the city felt so alive, filled with goodies. Afterward, I met my friend Laurie at St. John the Divine on the Upper West Side. This is one of the juxtapositions I love about life. In the morning I thought of Holocaust museums around the world, where I could send my book. In the afternoon, Divine intervention.

Laurie was intrigued by the musicians setting up for the next day's Sting concert. I was captured by the thought that I might be close to living my dream—to be read and known by those interested in the Holocaust, to show the aftermath from the eyes of the next generation.

I've been thinking about my next project, mostly because it feels good to have brought to fruition the one that was undone. I need to get more done—off the closet shelf so the work can become another thing that will enter the world.

While at St. John the Divine, I told Laurie that with my parents gone now, I could have a second life. She asked me what that meant. I said,

"No trauma, no pulling at me to forbid me the life I want." (Even though I'm not sure what that life looks like.) Iowa Tucson Albuquerque (and sometimes Pittsburgh) are never too far from mind. I added, "I want a relationship, but it's not a priority. Not now."

WRITING ABOUT MEMOIR

I'm teaching at a different school this semester. My two critical reading and writing classes there are struggling to get research papers done. Our course theme is "the recovery memoir." I selected three books for the class to dissect: Lauren Slater's *Prozac Diary*, Caroline Knapp's *Drinking a Love Story*, and Richard Cohen's *Blindsided: Lifting a Life above Illness*.

Students either love or hate the books that take us into Slater's journey on Prozac, Knapp's alcoholism, and Cohen's struggle with multiple sclerosis and cancer. There seems to be two prominent sides they're taking: one side feels that reading memoirs gives people hope—that they read them not voyeuristically, but to learn and be inspired. The other camp feels that we are all, in some way, attracted to other people's pain. By reading about other people's bad luck and challenges, we feel lifted about our own lives. I stand in the middle.

I can't say I've ever read a memoir and felt good about another's pain, but what I did feel was more accepting of my own. Reading about another person's life has at times broken through my walls of isolation. Writing about my life often does the same.

Why *do* people read memoirs? One guess is that readers look for themselves on the page, even when the writer's life is completely unlike theirs, even when they do read for a voyeur's thrill. For when we view a life unlike ours, we see ourselves more clearly. It's as though that other life frames us with its contrast.

I told my students they are making their research paper harder than it is. Not quite fair, for here I sit as grader, not a student, and I've had years of thinking about this very topic. And my thoughts about it are in constant flux.

I want my students to know whichever tack they take, they're on the right side.

MUSING

I imagine myself in the center of my family, bundled in warmth. I'm on the sofa with my father, separated by a checkerboard, the hum of a 1940s movie in the background—our favorites were musicals. And my mother, how she sings, her voice lilting from the kitchen through the apartment. My brother later reads a Tom and Jerry book to me. I'm seven, and this is the day I learn to write in script, scribbling *mmmmmm-mmmmmm* for miles. This is a wonderful day!

There was a time when I felt snug and blissful. As my brother and I got older and the American world entered our home with its choices, so far afield from my parents' shtetl lives, childhood bliss ended. In some way I will forever try to recapture that before period, that time of wanting for nothing.

Writing memoir is a handy way to travel back there. To draw a scene of the sofa and the checkerboard, and later, my brother, reading, handing me the pencil that carries my *mmmmmmmmmmmm*s to heaven and back.

A problem is that I get stuck in that place, forget that the "me" I'll write about in my memoir is a character, not the me of today. The me I am today at the Sunburst Espresso Bar, working on my laptop, sipping a café au lait, extra hot, has new choices, insight. I wonder how I'll fill my days when my book is done. (FYI, note "when" not "if.")

The semester is almost over. I'm always amazed when I make it through. I'll soon read the stack of papers, grade them, finish. And then, that wonderful, and at times frightening, tick-tock of time to write, and also to live away from the computer, to be in the world.

WHAT TO READ

I 'll soon have my first reading and signing of my essay collection at a local café. The essays I select to read will set the theme for the evening. My friend Debby tells me to steer clear of sad and depressing—in other words, the Holocaust. "Read the one about dieting," she says. "Everyone can relate." But what I really want is to read the one about my father, to transcend the sadness and pain of his passing.

My friend Rose reminds me the cover photo is of me and my mother, and that she encompasses so much of the work. Rose is right. It's my mother I should read about, my mother outside myself, on her stage, and the mother inside me, whom I often covet with the eyes of a three-year-old.

All the essays were written while she was alive, except the last, "The Unveiling." I wrote of my mother quite differently while she was alive than I did after. Perhaps for this reason, I'm shying away. I don't know that I was able to bring her fully to life, all the good and bad, while worrying she would read through me even when I (and my work) were fifteen hundred miles away from Florida.

Last night at a faculty Christmas party, while telling another writer about my book, I again realized so much of what I write isn't published. Yet, I call myself a writer; I identify myself (to myself) as such. And

I believe writing should be published, seen, read by others. That's my struggle: what is for an audience and what is just for me?

Maybe I'll talk about my mother and read about her, too. And while doing so I'll shift into her space, the one I was able to take when she relinquished the stage.

FYI, the café was crowded and lively with discussion. I had a flavorful taste of yes!

But, about yes . . .

I was a guest blogger on Poetica's site (my publisher—I love saying that). Guest blogging is a generous opportunity from the publisher for writers to spread their publicity wings and talk themselves up. But instead of writing about my essay anthology, I wrote about the pleasure of writing by hand and the yoga-ness of my peaceful rediscovery. In terms of writing about me in a way that sells books, that's tough stuff. My neighbor Jerry says I'm afraid to let myself feel successful.

I had a radio interview scheduled. I rehearsed the Q&As with Laurie and stumbled, stuttered, and then felt paralyzed. "I'm not ready," I told Laurie. "You never will be," she said. "Just do it." I wrote the station and I told the truth: I'm not ready for GO LIVE (as opposed to go live). Then, I breathed.

Today I received a book order from the United States Holocaust Memorial Museum in Washington, D.C. I am honored! Even though there is no such thing as bad publicity (so they say), I'm glad I put off the interview.

GETTING KNITTING

Now that grading is almost over, it's time to get honest about *Halfway Home*. Will I revise or file it away? Instead of facing the demon, I dig my knitting needles out of the closet and reach for the brown tweedy yarn; it will make a great hippie poncho with long fringes. My work today is not about breaking in the new computer or breaking apart old writing. Today, my work spills before me in rich color and texture and scratch.

There is a comfort in knitting, unlike the sweetness I find on my best writing days. Knitting asks nothing of me. I don't have to dig into memories and probe their deepest meanings. Knitting since I was seven, I hold decades of remembrances in my fingertips and in the feel of yarn wrapped around my finger.

Wool and the smells of lanolin, sheep, and long ago wintry days are all about sense memory. But while writing asks me to enter the feeling, take it down into its root, and then lift myself, knitting allows these sensory unravelings to hold me in place. That's not to say that knitting has never been about self-growth. I began a sweater business back in the 1980s, which I've never fully given up. There are always sweaters for sale around my place. And with each garment I've made, I've learned a new stitch, how to shape a sweater, write a pattern, mix yarns, market myself to crafts publishers and manufacturers, and so much more.

Then I became a writer. For the first five years of my writing career, writing was my sanctuary. And that included (and maybe was all about) the days I endlessly revised. Writing knocked knitting off my rung.

Later today, after getting the poncho going, I'll put the needles away and begin—for real—revising *Halfway Home*. I'll face the demon, the one I write and don't knit about.

But Enough about Me

Yesterday at Borders, I noticed that Julie Powell (of *Julie & Julia* fame) has a new memoir, *Cleaving: A Story of Marriage, Meat, and Obsession*. With a mixture of jealousy and curiosity, I wondered, how did she churn this out so quickly? Browsing through the book, I noted it's not a childhood whine, but rather a recent true story about her work as a butcher and her marital infidelity. The story looks quite—forgive me—juicy. Beyond that, I'm struck and intrigued because I long to write, as Powell does, of life in the present. (Or, of five years ago, tops.)

Mired in the past is how I feel, having begun the slow revision process of *Halfway Home*. One positive outcome—I discovered a forty-page gem within that I can turn into a work all its own. I'm considering a self-published chapbook. I'm comfortable with self-publishing, although I do wrestle with the kind of success I want.

Last week I caught myself in the act of looking to the outside for accolades. I received a book order that sent me flying with happiness, and I made some admirable PR moves. I had an interview in the *Brooklyn Daily Eagle*. There was also a generous review that said: *In her straightforward voice and gentle prose, Hurtes relates her struggle to move forward, while learning to move out from under the weight of her guilt. The essays are alternately funny and heartbreaking.* I crazily checked my emails for reader responses until I felt the insanity of my voracious need for recognition.

CLEARING OUT THE PAST

I'm always surprised when a plan I devise works as intended. The plan I refer to is the one to free myself, my hard drive, and the shelves in my closet of the past.

I'm going forward with the chapbook, hereafter known as *Rescue* (the title of my three shelved memoir drafts). I love my cover, *Flight of the Butterfly,* by artist Lori Goldberg. One part of the past I can check off the list.

I sent a link of the artwork to friends. Responses to the cover were divided. Gorgeous—corny. I wavered. But each time I gaze at the work, I'm immediately lost in the image of the graceful butterfly, illuminated in mist.

My mother is with me now, breathing, seeing herself in flight. In this way she and I were profoundly alike, longing for escape yet wavering at the open door.

For *Halfway Home* (hereafter known as *HH*) revisions, I'm expanding on the years when I was in graduate school—the years when I was a butterfly almost in flight to Iowa City Tucson Albuquerque (and sometimes Pittsburgh and only in my dreams Missoula). While in school, I was in the thick of regret and couldn't write about it with any perspective. Now, remembering, I wonder if the loneliness I felt in Brooklyn would have found me in places where the world is quiet. Or, would the very act of saying yes, fixed some broken part of me?

Soon I'll leave for a yoga class. In fact, I'm already there, with my decision to go. Yoga will work its magic, be one of my lifelines. Back at home, I'll return to the book and stick with it (I hope) until I find a new title. Until there's nothing halfway about my story.

Is It Possible to Get a Memoir Right?

There was a scene I'd written for *Rescue* where my parents had an argument over money. (My mother often complained that my father was cheap.) I liked the scene's energy and mood; but I was also uncomfortable with it. Because *Rescue* is relatively short, the scene didn't have any context supporting my mother's actions. And so I left the manuscript (which needed a good edit) on the side for a few days to get some distance. Upon my return and reading from cover to cover, I took out the scene, seeing it as gratuitous.

When working on my thesis in school, I worried about how people I wrote about would feel. That worry often guided my pen. I was aware that bowing to that worry was a major reason I hadn't produced a publishable book. If every memoirist fretted as I did, likely we would not be living in this age of memoir manna. Finding a compromise that doesn't muck up the truth hasn't been easy, but it is not, it appears, impossible. The story, as it is now, is tightly written with a focus on me and my mother, conveying an aspect of us that controls me until today. That aspect is ambivalence, which can paralyze me.

Like me, my mother had a divided self. She wanted to leap into success, and she wanted to find a way to do that, without the enormous guilt and burdens of her past. In fact my mother had "Iowa Tucson Albuquerque Pittsburgh" dreams too.

My parents' jewelry store was robbed four times, each time after they had closed at night. The fifth time was midday. They were tied up in the backroom of the store, threatened with guns.

They sold the business soon after. My father was at retirement age. My mother, still gorgeous, still vibrant, wanted to work at Tiffany's. She wanted to go places. From a poor village tucked into the Carpathian mountains to Fifth Avenue near the Plaza Hotel. She would have been fantastic.

And so after my parents retired, whenever I visited, my mother said, "I'm taking the Express Bus to Manhattan and getting a job at Tiffany's!" Then she'd look at my father for a response.

"You want to work at Tiffany's, work at Tiffany's," he'd say. Then he'd smile at me, a little Cheshire smile: *Do I care if she works at Tiffany's?*

"You should do it, Mom," I'd say. "You'd be great!"

By then my father had disappeared behind the newspaper. My mother rolled her eyes toward him, whispered to me, "He doesn't want me to."

Just across the street was the Express Bus. My mother could have had a life separate from us, far from home. Her Brooklyn was an immense distance from Fifth Avenue, the Plaza Hotel. Like my apartment in Brooklyn Heights: *How do we get across to the other side?*

I'll take the Express Bus. You'll see.

Eventually my mother stopped talking about Tiffany's, just as I stopped talking about Iowa and all the other places I didn't go.

⌣⌐

My hope is that in the chapbook, my mother appears as a flawed person and a victim of her history, rather than as a caricature. In my parents' passing, I realize their feelings about my book were never as much the issue as my own need to protect them.

The Act of Writing

As I write, I've got my eye on my pen, watching closely as it works its way across the page. Will it reveal something unexpected? A thought I didn't know I had begging for air? I hope so, because I spent a lot of time this week telling students, "Knowledge is hidden in your pen." For special effect, I held up a BIC and said, "You may not know what you have to say, but your pen does."

My lecture came straight from Sarah Porter's "The Pen Has Become the Character." This brilliant, award-winning article blows the whistle on teachers telling students that they should know what to write before they even start. Rather, Porter says, tell students their writing will show them what's there to be written.

In English composition classes, many students struggle with the questions: *How do I begin? I know what I want to say, but how do I write it?* I tell them to write what they think the answer to their research question might be, to pick up the pen and start: *If I had to guess at the answer I'd say . . .* or *I chose this research question because . . .* If they give up self-consciousness, their pen will lead them. In their eyes, that's good and bad. They might discover something that takes them in an unintended direction. For a research paper, that can mean abandoning hours of work already done. The limited time built into a syllabus to write a paper can make exploration with a pen a luxury.

This week I put myself in poetry-writing mode and wrote, *I didn't know when my father died he'd leave my heart undone. The silence of my grief is deafening.* Words fell easily to the page, and yet, I stopped. So much work to do—papers to read, rosters, progress reports, agendas. But the real reason I stopped is that I didn't want to face what my pen told me: how much I miss my father.

Sarah Porter says our self takes shape on the page. I feel that statement viscerally. When allowing the wonder and beauty of words to transcend my censors, I feel as if I'm flying. And I discover what's in my heart: *I didn't know when my father died he'd leave my heart undone. The silence of my grief is deafening.*

TELLING TRUE STORIES

I n last semester's critical reading and writing classes, we had a speak-er from the publishing industry. Class discussion quickly got around to Mackenzie Phillips and her memoir, *High on Arrival*. We tossed around the question: was writing about her incestuous relationship with her father necessary for her to move past it? Our speaker pointed out that by promoting the book, the experience is Phillips's present day. That could make moving past the trauma difficult.

Would it be better, then, to write the thing, put it under the bed, and walk away, over and done? A few years ago I interviewed a writer who'd written a memoir on a similar theme. She said that writing about the experience enabled her to gain control over it. Publishing turned it into art and a way to help others. She never regretted it.

Now that *Rescue* is published, I contribute copies to Holocaust mu-seums and college libraries. I breathe a deep sigh of relief. Not just in being finished with that material; it's also as though "that material" about my mother and me is now the past.

After a memoir is published, what we do with it is a personal choice. Just as memoir is not merely what happened, but what we make of what happened, so too is the finished product. Do we now cry or try to shock people while discussing our book, because we need something from them? Or do we continue to grow through the process?

I often wonder if I'd be better off working in a jazzy ad agency, away from me, but still creative.

LIVING IN THE PROCESS

*O*n *My Way to Someplace Else* received a wonderful review from the *Midwest Book Review.* They called it ". . . a top pick for memoir collections." When I read those words, I felt a sense of completion. The validation I seek arrived, fit itself neatly inside me.

I imagine everyone who receives a great review feels wonderful. But for all of us, that burst of pleasure is likely for different reasons. Getting a self-published book reviewed is no easy task. The process has been one of sending out books, waiting, and hoping. Then the review came, and in a blink I had arrived on the platform I had always wanted to stand on, but couldn't climb up to. Someone else's words became my stepladder.

I'd like to think that arrival happens the moment the project begins. Sitting at the computer day after day, pulling up words when they don't come easily, endlessly revising, tolerating so much alone time—all the behind-the-scenes work. In yoga class, the teacher reminds us, *Don't think about the next pose while you're in the one you're in now.* She gives alternate poses so that students can adjust their practice for themselves. *When you're in a pose because someone else is in it, you're no longer practicing yoga.*

My physical release into the poses has deepened. My practice begins while waiting for the bus; the forty minutes it takes to get to the yoga studio is part of the discipline.

I treasure my great book review. But what if it had not been good? Today, I'll try practicing yoga when I return to an unfinished project, put a sticker on my computer screen that reads, *I've arrived*.

BURNING THINGS

I t's always a relief to focus on topics outside myself. But, it's also true that when swept along in someone else's story, I find myself.

In O'Brien's *The Things They Carried*, the character Jimmy Cross is a platoon leader in Vietnam. He's obsessed with Martha, a girl whose letters he continuously reads. While he's thinking of Martha, a soldier is shot and dies. Cross ultimately burns Martha's letters out of guilt and a desire to buck up and live in the present moment.

My present moment wobbles, like when I'm in tree pose. I lose my *drishti*.

I had a friend who kept a journal where she wrote about the past. That was her way of taming the beast, keeping regrets and guilt away from her real life. That worked for her for a long time. But the notebooks, so full from her stories, were crowded inside her night table; they woke her with their clamors for release. It was time to burn them, she said.

At the time, I kept a journal of my dreams; as soon as I woke, I jotted down images—men I'd been involved with, airplanes and forests, a house in upstate New York that I often visited in my sleep. But the story these images told were indecipherable during the day. My friend invited me to a "bonfire of the insanities." I smiled at the image of us taking our notebooks to a park, lighting a fire, dancing as every single word burned.

Perhaps courage is making a choice—not a perfect one, but the best one—even if it's to absolve guilt as it was for O'Brien's Jimmy Cross.

DISAPPOINTMENT

An editor who'd written me a glowing email with a heads-up that he would write a similar review for my essay collection, didn't. I checked the newspaper, my sales, my email, hoping to see some sign. But none came. It took a lot for me to follow up with him and ask if the review was still on the calendar.

Not right now, he wrote back. *I'll stay in touch.*

When *On My Way to Someplace Else* first came out, I sent copies to editors who had published my essays as individual pieces. I didn't yet know how hard it would be to get reviewed. This editor's email made me think that getting publicity for a self-published work would be easy. In fact, I went so far as to see my humble book—soft cover, small press— as the little book that could.

Moving around in the publishing world has always been difficult for me. My most comfortable place is at the keyboard, surrounded by others in a noisy café. And so I tried ignoring my need to ask the editor why. I paused—sort of. I didn't pause so that I could ask in a way that wasn't whiny or hurt (it felt like a breakup). I paused because I didn't think I was entitled to know. But without knowing, not only did my brain create awful scenarios, but I felt erased.

I must've woken up the next morning from confident dreams, because I sent off a short, kind, and questioning note. *I'm excited about my forthcoming review. Do you have a publish date for it?* I felt resolved. Then I posted to my blog about the situation, and wouldn't you know, right after I checked my email, there was an answer. *We're reestablishing our mission. I'll let you know.* In plain English: No dice.

I'll never know why the review won't run, but it is safe to say that it won't. That's not the most important part of this story. What I take from it is that it's my right to ask why, regardless of whom I'm interacting with. Asking why reveals that I care, and that is something I've long been embarrassed to show in my business and personal life.

I was disappointed. Perhaps the reason to have unfinished manuscripts around is that I can turn to them for solace. I went back to *Halfway Home*:

During the war, my father was in five labor camps. He told me the names of the camps when, as an adult, I asked. But the names and the cities with consonants strung together formed clumsy sounds and were impossible for my American ears to decipher, for my daughterly heart to assimilate.

I discovered, also as an adult, my father's sister Sylvia had watched their parents Leibich and Miriam walk into the ovens at Auschwitz. I knew that Wolf, Herschel, and Mendel were also killed in the ovens. David, the youngest, was a missing person. His name wasn't on the lists of the dead; he was last seen in Budapest. My father's brother Moishe survived; but his wife and two young sons were killed.

My father never spoke to me of his grief. Only as an adult did I ask, "How did you go on?"

"It vas terrible, of course. Not just for me, for everyone. But vat else could ve do? Ve did the best ve could."

My father's simple lesson—we did the best we could—would mingle with my mother's yearning for a life beyond her grasp, and form the backbone of who I was—a woman who lived simply but so very complicatedly.

DAYBREAK

I have no classes today; still, I'm out at 6:00 a.m., emptying my palate of the lingering taste of dreams. Outdoors, half a block from my apartment building, I walk up a long concrete staircase leading to the parks. I run into a neighbor. She tells me she's moving home to Sri Lanka, where she has a house, large enough to contain ten Tudor City studios. But it is not the comfort of that largesse that lures her; she can't find work, here, in Manhattan.

She puts her hands out on either side of her body, like scales. "Move to Queens?" she says, lowering her left. "Sri Lanka?" Her right hand rises. "I lived in Jackson Heights for three years," she says, "and was lonely and depressed. But I can't afford to live in Manhattan."

I nod, thinking, *I can't either. But Manhattan is good to single people.*

Last night at dinner with my friend Stephanie, I listened with a mixture of envy and pleasure as she described her Sunday mornings. *By 6:00 I'm on my deck, with a mug of Earl Grey.* I pictured her in her Secaucus condo, surrounded by trees, leaves dotted with morning dew, her palm warm and steamy.

Today I want to live in the country. Inhale the scent of grass and late night rain. I want to walk barefoot in the damp grass. I want to hang my laundry outside on a line to dry, have wooden clothespins in a basket.

Then the city announces itself. Buses, taxis, people on their way to work. I plan my day: shop for cute tops for yoga, hit Starbucks afterwards with a heap of student papers and a café au lait, extra hot and foamy.

But where will I move if my landlord, Laura, calls to tell me she's not renewing my sublease? Will I by default end up where I don't want to be? Am I destined to live a by-default life?

I take out the Windex and paper towels, remove the three potted coleus from the sills, clean my windows.

THE BIG PICTURE

One of my students is being deployed; another is joining the military. When they told me, I saw those young men whose expressions usually seem to say, *I'd rather be anywhere but in your class*, as boys I wanted to protect. I also saw how easy it is to misinterpret my students' nuances and expressions—falling asleep in class means I'm boring, not they were up all night working at a second (or third) job.

In one-to-one conferences, I read pages of students' journals. When I was young, I had little privacy away from mother's eyes. I kept my diary in my pajama drawer. I wrote cautiously in my diary, kept it because that's what girls did, not because I needed to write my secret thoughts. Knowing my mother had free access to my thoughts, I gave that diary nothing.

And so I tell students I never read through journals. They place a paper clip on the entries I can read. I wonder if they do this purposefully: one student wrote about being overwhelmed by a class lesson. I sighed deeply, the way I always do when taking in a truth. I thanked her for showing me that; I made a mental note: discuss assignments piece by piece. In the English Department at my CUNY school, this is referred to as "scaffolding," wherein small assignments lead up to the larger, big picture.

In an in-class writing exercise last week, students' dreams trickled to the page. I asked them to write a tentative introduction for their research paper. When I called on students to read, one read the opening to what could become a beautiful poem. He was embarrassed he hadn't done what he was supposed to. He said, "This is what my pen wrote." We applauded. For that moment, the big picture—or rather, *my* big picture—was meaningless.

When we allow the writing process to take hold, the pen reveals its own mind. But, of course, at some point, that introduction must be written, poetry put aside. The pen controlled. At least, that's the way it works in my academic writing classes. I give students the basic essay formula: five paragraphs, including an introduction and conclusion; the thesis is the last sentence(s) of the intro, quotations integrated in a "quotation sandwich" (a phrase I wish I'd made up, but in fact, stole): *Your own words are the bread; they introduce the quote. The quote is the tuna fish. Then your own words again explain the quote.* And a conclusion with a "takeaway" (phrase stolen, too, from NPR).

REMEMBERING

This has been my week of sleeping badly in anticipation of today. The morning's television news is all about Father's Day. My plan for today is to go to a yoga class and begin an essay "Why I Write." *Poets & Writers* magazine has a column on this topic, which asks, "Why in the face of rejection or other challenges, do you continue to write?"

Today, the "why" is that I write to remember my father, before and even during his stroke. I write to feel his presence, to say hello and good-bye again. I write to have this day in the best way I can. My feelings flow through my arms to my fingertips. They gather on my pillow. I inhale the scent of *Old Spice*.

The Temple of Life

I'm reading *Eat, Pray, Love*, by Elizabeth Gilbert. I spurned this book for years, and the reason? Jealousy. Jealous I wasn't living an "eat pray love" life, jealous I hadn't written that book. But in three weeks I'm going to Tuscany! This is a trip I've wanted to take for years. When my mother died, I left Brooklyn. In my father's death, I settle into another departure. Nine days in Florence and the Tuscan countryside and twenty-four hours in Rome. But unlike Gilbert, my trip is not one of self-exploration. It is Italy the easy way: group tour, deluxe hotels, meals included, bus excursions, lunch in a palace!, two days to ourselves. When our nine days are up, I'll remain in Rome while the group returns to the United States.

In Gilbert's section "Pray," she writes about choosing her thoughts. She acknowledges how hard it is, but that it is possible. That's not the first time I've read or heard this premise, but when I do, it's always new and reassuring. And in an important way that's what writing is for me, especially when I travel outside my comfort zone.

The pen in my hand is familiar; it takes me home regardless of where I am; it gives me a break from my whirlwind of thoughts.

Pen. Home. Grace into stillness.

LOOSE ENDS

The past two weeks have been a push/pull between my teaching and writing lives. Having returned to *Halfway Home*, I surprised myself by getting involved in the story of the places I didn't go and the one I did.

Emily had gone to Iowa City and Albuquerque to check out the schools, after we received our acceptance letters. She called me from the road: I'd just had a facial at a fancy East Side salon. I was having lunch at a coffee shop on East 57th Street with a high school friend and her twenty-eight-year old daughter.

"Emily!" I said, dying to hear everything.

"I'm in Iowa!" she said, and we burst out laughing. I whispered across the table, "It's my friend who I'm going to school with." My friend at the table smiled and talked with her daughter about going to Bloomingdale's to shop for an evening dress. The world entering me through my cell phone—intellectual and vibrant—made me feel alive. The world across from me—financially secure, responsible, age-appropriate—was what I wanted too.

My heart pounding, I said, "I'll be fifty-five when school starts. What will I do in Iowa City? Who will I date? If I were your age I'd go. You have to go."

"Sandy, you'll do what we'll all do. You'll make the best of it."

I mumbled something like, "You're right. Yes, I'll do it."

You know the rest. Ironically, one of my New York City classmates had come to my school from where else? Iowa.

It seems I can revise forever. Each time, I reveal deeper levels of understanding. While writing about the time I sat with my friend and talked on the phone to Emily, I realize I didn't want my friend's life. Not her daughter, not her expensive Upper East Side co-op. But I was terrified of the loneliness of stepping off the age-appropriate path, terrified of my own desires.

A memory comes to me:

It was a summer in the Catskills, 1960. My family went to a bungalow colony every summer; 50 percent of the population was Holocaust survivor families. We always went to a different colony. We followed along with family, my parents' friends, and tried new places that had popped up. I said good-bye to my city friends. I wandered around the first days, lonely and deeply sad. Then my mother took me by the hand, walked me over to girls my age, introduced me. Then I was okay.

One day I was by myself on the swings. I held the chains of my swing and pumped. *Higher. Higher.* I had seen the teenage girls pumping hard, their bodies jutting forward then back, their hair flying. Gangly boys had stood nearby and watched. I felt grown-up and alive. *Higher. Higher.* My ponytail swung behind me. I saw my father in the distance, his beveled silhouette. "Daddy!" I waved. *Higher still.* And then my heart froze as my swing hovered, level with the top bar. For a few seconds I went blank. Then I clutched the chains, terrified, as I swung back down.

My father neared. My heart palpitated. Maybe my father took me by the hand and said, "Let's go." Or reprimanded me: "Don't go so high." I don't remember what he did. I prayed he hadn't seen me. As we walked back to our bungalow, I was flooded with guilt and shame for trying to be the free teenage girl that I was not.

Today, I met my friend Debby, who loaned me her travel yoga mat. As she handed me the piece of cloth that would bring me peace, she said to be careful in Florence: "It has the highest crime rate in the country." Another friend had told me to wear my passport on a string around my neck.

Are they afraid I'll go *over* the bar?

(FYI, Florence does *not* have the highest crime rate. I will *not* wear my passport like a necklace.)

BEFORE AND AFTER

Now I stand beneath an umbrella and gaze at an ancient, massive structure, otherwise known as the Pantheon. Throngs of people walk in clusters headed by tour guides. I'm a pedestrian today, not a tourist. I want to look and stroll and *not* see it all.

The most moving part of my trip to Italy: my free day when I walked through the city of Lucca. The old-world stone streets and buildings reminded me of photos I'd seen of my ancestors' homes. The city had a haze to it, like an architectural drawing of an idea that has not fully colored itself in. The Tuscany countryside was breathtaking; it stoked fantasies from when I'd seen *Under the Tuscan Sun*. In the movie, an American woman bought a house, had fabulous sex, cooked, and fell in love. But it was in Lucca my heart saw through the haze, colored in the lines.

During my nine days—not intended for meditation or self-reflection— I felt wonderfully complete. I had made it to Italy after years of yearning. The town of Montecatini, our nine-day home base, was hilly and "happening." Lots of bars, cafés, shops.

One rainy morning I sat in my room and chanted: *Home.* The sound reverberated in my throat. The hum felt good as it seeped through my nostrils, down my throat, out my nostrils again. As a seeker of a

happiness that I think is out there, somewhere, it had never before occurred to me that my mantra could be home. And . . . it never occurred
to me that the infamous "om" is right there, in home.

I left the safety net of my group at Leonardo da Vinci Airport; they
headed toward TWA and their flight back to the States. I wheeled my
forest-green Samsonite past ticket counters and families speaking in a
rush of Italian. I asked everyone I passed, "Termini Station?" I followed
their gazes to distant passageways, elevators, crowds. I found the train,
settled into my window seat, smiled at the blur of low-level buildings
connected with clotheslines; shirts, sheets, trousers waved.

I was reminded of another trip I took alone, thirty years before—an
Eat Pray Love kind of trip to Greece and Israel—filled with adventures
in which I drank tequila with strangers in an olive field, slept on the
beach in Corfu (also with strangers—but then, strangers are the point
of traveling alone), slept in a kibbutz (yes, with a stranger) ten miles
from the Lebanese border (at a time of war).

Now I head for Trevi Fountain. Maybe I'll bump up against a handsome stranger; we'll sip cappuccino, kiss the foam off each other's lips.
Could I find the space here, in Rome, to be an "us" yet remain the me I
know myself to be?

The bells of Saint Something are ringing.

Not Forcing Things

I joined a real yoga studio. I hate to admit it, but yoga there has elevated my practice from my classes at the Y. I'd like to think yoga is what I allow it to be, regardless of where I practice—and quite likely it is. But I'm not in that evolved Zen mindset.

The new studio on the Upper East Side has six levels of classes (Introduction, Gentle, Level 1, Level 1/2, Level 2/3, Level 3), not one size fits all, common at Ys. Teachers have five hundred hours of training as opposed to the two hundred required for certification.

I like the intense focus on alignment. I learned, for example, that a way to measure the V of my downward dog is to start in extended child pose. The tip of my fingers to the press of my toes is my length. When I move into a V, my hands and feet remain in place.

I'm learning to respect props—items that once made me feel inadequate. Each has the purpose of helping me take care of myself. Blankets beneath my knees during corpse pose protect my back; my palms on blocks during lunges protect my back and shoulders; looping a belt around my foot in seated forward bend gives me a wonderful hamstring stretch, protects my back, and helps my alignment.

Relating self-care to my life is far more difficult. For writing, that means no second-guessing decisions made in the past (even million-$$$

book deals). Then, there's my teaching life. The nature of being an adjunct feels very non-yoga. There's the hourly teaching rate, which never compensates fairly for the actual hours spent planning, reading, grading, and assorted administrative tasks. I can't breathe away my dissatisfaction; I can't notice it without getting upset.

At the business college—a serious offender of unpaid time—I've set up a meeting with my Chair to discuss a salary review. To prepare I must separate my emotion from the facts of why I deserve the raise. Am I trying to change school rules so that unpaid time becomes illegal for adjuncts, or get myself compensated? In truth, both. But what is more possible?

I pick up a pen and paper—my most available and loyal props—which allow me to write out the injustice, my fury.

IN MOVEMENT

My landlord left me a voice mail. Laura will be in town with her daughter, Amy, to see a play. *Can we stop by? I'd love to see how the apartment looks without the carpet.* She lives not far in New Jersey, but we've never met. My first thought was, *Oh no, she's going to want the apartment back.* My second, *Good, she's going to want the apartment back.*

I called Laura. *Yes, of course.* After all, it's her apartment.

I'm nursing a low-level anxiety. It's easy (and fun) to have a wild and restless *drishti* while I have a signed sublease. But when I no longer have one, I fear, I'll be a ten-year-old, pumping too high on the swings.

⟲

Laura and Amy came over carrying a *Playbill* from a Broadway musical. We kissed and hugged as if we were old friends. Laura remembered the apartment her parents had once lived in. She loved the way I had my desk beneath a cabinet in a corner, and the pine counter with stools that separated the kitchen area from the rest of the room.

I felt proud for keeping the studio clean and painted. I wanted them to love the place, as if they were my parents who had come for an inspection.

Amy spotted my yoga mat leaning against the wall.

"I do yoga!" she said.

"Oh . . . yeah . . . I really like it."

"Is there a studio nearby?" she asked.

"Yoga is all over . . . the Y . . . even free in Bryant Park."

I pointed to the space where I placed my open mat and the two-foot-wide wall space where I had enough room for "legs up the wall."

Maybe I wanted them to love the apartment so they *would* take it back, so I would have to go someplace—live my Iowa dreams.

In a telephone conversation two weeks later, Laura confirms it: "Amy is ready to be launched." I have ten months to find a place to live.

Non-Doing

I've been reading *Wherever You Go There You Are*, by Jon Kabat-Zinn. In spite of the corniness of the title, the book jumped out at me each time I saw it on a bookshelf. I finally bought it and am reading it slowly, digesting each page, every one holding treasures of wisdom.

Kabat-Zinn writes about the concept of non-doing. I won't try to paraphrase him, because I'll surely screw it up. But my interpretation of non-doing is that it's not sitting and waiting for things to happen. Rather, it's not forcing things to go my way.

My new yoga studio has several locations throughout the city (actually the country). But with my reduced membership as a teacher (had I mentioned that enticement away from the Y?), I can only go to one studio. That forced me to make a choice: at the Upper East Side studio there's a teacher who incorporates yogic philosophy. But she is only there once a week. There's a studio close to my apartment where I go more frequently. I chose the latter because I love walking to yoga. I've been missing that teacher, but I couldn't bring myself to transfer my membership.

Last Saturday, while reading Kabat-Zinn's book and waiting for class, I heard a few students complain that my current yoga studio was closing. Everyone had to choose a new location. A crowd of dissidents formed (in a yoga studio!). They want *that* space. It's so large, sunny, close to everything. While listening, I had never felt so peaceful and smug as I felt that moment. I was on my way back to my beloved teacher, and I hadn't done a thing. Non-doing in perfect symmetry.

Non-doing is much harder when the stakes are higher. Like not paying attention to who is (and isn't) buying my essay collection, not ruminating on Iowa Tucson Albuquerque (and sometimes Pittsburgh)—and now where to move. That's tough stuff. I'm comfortable in those mental trips that I compulsively take. That's likely why I was so attracted to Kabat-Zinn's subject. He reminds me that these exhausting habits take me away from a sustaining sense of peace.

I looked at a studio on the far Upper East Side. It was on the fourth floor of a walk-up. (I've been spoiled by my elevator building with concierge.)

Note to self: figure out how to apply "non-doing" to finding a place—the perfect place—to live.

More than Reading and Writing?

I'm wondering how I can apply my newly found "non-doing" philosophy to my teaching life. Right after the official last day when a student can withdraw from class without penalty, absent students appeared with excuses and promises in hand, tears ready to spill.

The non-doing seems easy. Their extensive absences and missed assignments equal failure, as stated on the syllabus. Yet in the faculty room, conversations ensue. Going by the book (aka syllabus) is often hard on teachers. Students aren't purposefully screwing up—there's stuff going on in their lives. And the pleading look in their eyes . . . ouch.

In my early teaching days, a C student told me she needed a B to continue getting financial aid. I suddenly wasn't just a composition teacher, but a student of ethics. I talked to a friend who is an experienced teacher. She pointed me to an article—just that week—in the *New York Times*, by the Ethicist, Randy Cohen. He'd received a letter from a teacher with my exact dilemma. He wrote something to the effect of, actions have consequences. It was the student, not me, who should take the fall. So, there you go. Cause and effect.

Yesterday, a student proposed, for her last paper, a campaign against attendance policies. Her reasoning: if she's completed all her work and received As, but then takes one too many absences, her grade will drop. She wants to know, what does that prove about her abilities? Maybe nothing; but I need to believe class time is important. Otherwise, why bother?

Teachers are far from grading robots—we often sweat these issues out. Bottom line: failing a student sucks. In the imperfect and complicated world of the classroom, non-doing takes a thrashing.

Internal Landscapes

I'm reading an article in *Yoga Journal* about how meditating can re-structure the brain. My understanding is that, simply put, we become what we focus on. Although this seems obvious, the idea strikes me as profound, particularly so because I spend a lot of time rummaging through the past. This thinking/writing about the past populates my life with a lot of ghosts who infringe upon the happiness I stumble upon in the present.

In my late twenties, I wanted to be a travel and adventure writer—not as in taking to the high seas or exploring underwater fauna, but as in "single woman out in the world" adventures. Yet I soon developed a fear of flying—literally. I didn't board a plane for ten years and took few car or train trips. And therein my writing career took shape—figuring out the push/pull between my yearning to leap into the world and utter reluctance to do so. For better or worse, I've had tons of material. I never seem to get exhausted plumbing my life's anxieties. But I am getting bored.

I'm wondering if it's not too late to have those travel adventures. What would my brain reshape itself into, if I spent my days and writing time romancing the present? I think this is all a long-winded way of saying that I did more work on *Halfway Home*.

My mother's warm breath seems to tickle my ear; the scents of her Dentyne and dime-store lipstick rise up my nostrils.

"You'll zug gurnish, mámala, tell no one, you hear?"

The years go by like a train speeding through stations. 1957. '56. '55. We're seated on the wide bulky chair in the apartment on Union Street.

"When Hitler came to our village, he sent us on a train to Auschwitz," my mother said, only she sounded like this: trrrain to Ausch-vitz.

"There were two lines formed. One for death, one for labor. I was on the selection line with my sisters Surika and Sharika. They were so skinny, like little sticks, like nothings. And I was plump. What would the Germans need my sisters for? They couldn't work, they couldn't lift heavy machinery.

A few feet away from us is my parakeet, Pokey. Unwitting witness to the unfolding of my mother's life, his yellow-gold beak twitching forward and back.

"You know what would become of them? Death."

A square dirt yard, the circumference of a schoolyard, a row of women dressed in rags, barefoot, hairless. Another row of fleshy women, their bodies bulging with life.

"The SS looked up and down the lines, knowing that the skinny ones with their ribs protruding were useless. But the SS didn't know who they were dealing with. You understand, mámala?"

My mother has ways of getting through the worst circumstances.

"My mother didn't give birth to a nar, a fool. Surika's name was called. She was so skinny I knew what would happen to her. I pulled her back and stepped off the selection line in her place. One look at me, with my fat cheeks, and he shouted 'Labor!' I pushed Suri in the direction of the labor line.

"Then he called out for Sharika. Again, I stepped forward before he could send her to death. 'Labor!' he said, barely lifting his head. I pushed her to stand with Suri.

"What did he know? With a quick look, all of us with no hair, we looked the same. Then he called me.

"'Rifka!'

"I came forward. I stood as still as I could, although I was shivering in the cold. This time he looked at me from my filthy bare feet to my face.

"My sisters were huddled together watching. Then when he was good and ready, he gave his order. 'Labor!'

"If not for me, Símala, my sisters would be dead."

My mother's head on my shoulder. I tap her on the back the way she taught me. Soft touches as her mother did for her.

Tap tap tap.

"Símala scheina, you are my reason."

My mother called me her reason; but when I look back now, I see her reason was her survival. That was the one constant in her life that never abandoned her. For my mother to let her survival go would have been complete submission to the horror she'd lived through.

It wasn't me keeping my mother alive. It was she, pumping her own heart, her own blood. But I couldn't have known that as a young girl, and apparently, I couldn't have known it until now, this minute. I valued my place too much in my mother's life, her place in mine to question or wonder.

I treated my mother's life preciously, held it in my palms as if it were glass.

What to Read, Again

I n my teaching life, I'm drawn to literature populated by characters with messy, conflicted lives. Some of my students are groaning about being on the receiving end of this. In one of my classes, we're reading Khaled Hosseini's *The Kite Runner*. Themes of friendship, betrayal, and redemption provide us with great class discussions. But my students—most of whom haven't yet gotten to the good stuff in the book—are immersed in the sad worlds of war and disloyalty.

Past experience sneaks up at the most unlikely moments. When I select my texts, my past guides me. In *The Kite Runner* we meet Amir, a young man haunted by guilt for betraying his friend; my students almost always hate Amir. I try to help them see that we all make at least one terrible choice as a child; one of mine was rejecting my best friend after my family moved from Crown Heights to Flatlands.

At twelve-step meetings where you can hear all sorts of wonderful slogans, they say, "Look back but don't stare." I like that. It tells me to see how yesterday can affect tomorrow. But I don't have to make it my tomorrow.

For my own pleasure, I often read to be carried away by a good story—and it doesn't always have to be poetically written. I love page-turning thrillers and romantic (but not romance) novels. I read Harlan

Coben's thriller *Tell No One* in 2003, after my mother died. I distracted myself from my grief with books that grabbed my attention in a way most other things couldn't. I also liked the opening: a man receives an email from his "deceased" wife. Technology was still young, at least in my life. And so the inclusion of the Internet in a novel intrigued me.

Luanne Rice's *Home Fires* is one of my favorite beach reads. A woman recovering from the loss of her daughter falls in love with an equally wounded, and scarred, firefighter. Each time I read the book, I fall in love with him, too. And quite likely, even in my "fun" read, I find an echo of my past—seeing my father in the firefighter in need of comfort.

My challenge as a teacher is to help students tap their own pasts when reading a novel or when writing a story of their own.

A Spirited Pause

I'm going to slightly distort a quote I heard in last night's yoga class, which was something like "Form is of the spirit, product of the ego." I reflected on how stunningly that phrase relates to writing.

When I don't compare myself to authors whose bound books are piled on the tables at Borders, I feel accomplished. But it's so easy to focus on product. Ego stuff. I want to say that it's the culture that drives me to think beyond what satisfies my soul. That may be true, but it's also true that something within me seeks external rewards.

I read an entry on a well-published novelist's website. She wrote that if you're not publishing your work, you're not a writer. I flinched. Perhaps her words were too close to my bone, or maybe I vehemently disagree.

Well-Published Novelist (WPN) lives in Philadelphia. My cousins live in the suburbs right outside the city. They would love to help me find an apartment (lower rent, for certain) and make me part of their daily lives.

Maybe WPN and I would be friends. I'd tell her, very courteously, that I disagree with her statement. And she, very courteously, would ask, what am I hiding from?

And I would think, *why is she being provocative in* my *fantasy?*

*T*his is how I feel about writing: It's not fair to place it on a higher plateau than any other meaningful endeavor. It's been years since I knit for a living, but I'm still a first-class knitter. When I lose myself in the feel of yarn unfurling through my fingers and the design, which seems to happen on its own, I'm completely of the spirit. And that's always a good place for me to be.

HERE AND THERE

M y teaching life these days feels scattered. My summer course was cancelled; I lament my life as an adjunct. I'm considering learning web design . . . retail . . . and Very Seriously considering taking the two-hundred-hour yoga teacher training. Coursework in philosophy, postures, and anatomy could fill the spaces in my helter-skelter teaching life. And if anything sounds like a road to peace that would be it: immersion in yogic philosophy and ancient teachings.

My writing life feels scattered, too. Maybe that's because I'm still revising *HH*.

My mother and her sisters Sharika and Surika woke up on a morning in April 1945 and found themselves in an eerily quiet bunk. No SS barking, Mach schnell! *"Hurry up!" No shuffling feet of the SS walking up and down the yard, their guns poised. No smoke coming in from the crematorium.*

My mother rose from her cot and with the others searched the barracks. "We were on tippy toe, looking all over, even in the showers. There was no one. Nothing. Not one SS bitch." The door to their bunk was open. They peered outside, into the yard and saw the barbed-wire fence had been cut; the dirt road without the sprays of dust the guards kicked up on their daily marches. Without a connection to one of the underground news sources that many Jews in hiding tapped into, the women in the barracks had no knowledge that the war had ended. They knew only that there was an uncanny silence.

Still, the women didn't step outside. In the distance, trucks swayed as if they'd tip over on the rock-strewn road. Packed inside were men in uniforms, shrieking in Russian, Te svebodna! "You're free!" The trucks came closer. The soldiers jumped off the trucks before they had even stopped; they ran into the bunk; they laughed, they sobbed.

My mother slid into a corner, stood numb against the wall. Her burlap uniform hung from her skeletal frame. She was seventeen years old, skin and bones. A handsome soldier was drawn toward her. He lifted my mother off the ground, danced her around the bunk. When he put her down he kissed her cheeks and told her, Ti krasivaja! "You're beautiful!"

My mother then stumbled through the open door. The women piled out behind her, insane with joy and disbelief. They ran to the commissary. There they found all the food sealed in cans, except for mustard. Barrels and barrels of mustard, which my mother loved. She cupped her hands and dipped them in the barrel, drinking the thick liquid-like soup. Her stomach distended. The others went outside and found a wagon hitched to a horse. They hollered, "Rifka!" She was rolling on the floor in pain. The women carried her from the commissary and lifted her onto the wagon.

The wagon crowded with women seemed to soar through the camp, down the dirt road. All along the roads were abandoned houses that only the day before had been filled by Germans. The women stopped and went into a house. Before looking for food, they stripped the curtains off the windows. They tore their uniforms off and wrapped the fabric around their bodies like sarongs, covered their bald heads with turbans.

In the Russian soldier's arms, and then again wrapped in the chintz fabric, my mother realized the beautiful woman she had somehow become.

Dear Past,
I still need you to finish this book. But you're being put on notice. I'm getting ready to break up with you ("getting ready" are the operative words). I'm getting pumped up about opening closets and drawers, shooing away your spirits.

Dear Self,
Do not turn moving into a major trauma.

But Where?

In the early 1990s, when I read the novel *Anywhere but Here*, I felt a visceral connection to the title. I wasn't yet a working writer. But still. Author Mona Simpson had snatched the book's title from my future grasp.

I'm having an anywhere-but-here kind of day. This perfect summer Sunday yearns for me to be elsewhere. (If a Sunday can yearn, that is.) The day began like this: I walked a half mile to a yoga class. Stretched, twisted, and respected my limitations (aka bulging disc). So far, so good. On the way back, I planned the smoothie I'd concoct when I got home. In between inventorying my freezer—strawberries, blueberries—then the fridge—wheat germ, flax seed, milk—this thought nudged its way in: *where should I be today*? Not as in, for the day, like Jones Beach or the Jersey Shore—but for my life. Philadelphia? Tucson? Queens?

Why do such questions come to me on perfect summer Sundays after yoga? My mind is a gypsy. Last night I went to a networking event. I met a doctor who invited me on a mission to Haiti. *Haiti? How about a tiny town in Alaska?* (Have I mentioned my childhood obsession with igloos?) *No. Haiti.*

This gypsy wants to set the time and place. Friends of a friend are working for Habitat for Humanity. Maybe I'll go with them. Certainly, if they go to Alaska. (And absolutely positively yes if it involves an igloo.)

TECHNIQUE

I once thought it was possible to mimic another writer's style. Carolyn Knapp's *Drinking: A Love Story* is one of my favorite memoirs. I read it several times to study her style. And then I taught the book. With all those reads, I could pick up the book today and still be mesmerized. Knapp's writing is urgent, as if she needs to write the next page and the next, as eager as the reader to find out where her story goes. She *seems to be asking, Will I end up okay at the end?*

That energy, that fury, keeps me hooked, even though I know the end. There are some places in *HH* where I pull off something similar. One section, besides my mother's story of saving her sisters at the line-ups, involves receiving the acceptance letters from the MFA programs. Did I mention that I had tried to say yes to Iowa?

I wrote an email: *Thank you for accepting me into Iowa's nonfiction program. I can't wait to start . . .* I wanted my reply to be perfect so I saved the email as a draft. Over the next days I opened it, edited, saved, and on and on, until the deadline drew near. *This is it,* I told myself, then tried to hit "send." My finger would not click on the mouse. I called Emily and left a message: *Call me!* I had a glass of wine, took deep breaths, tried to hit "send" again . . . I could not. I visualized the scene: I imagined clicking "send" and tried to picture myself happy. But I could not get to happy, not when I felt the blood drain from my body.

Ultimately, I wrote to Iowa: *I've decided to go to school in New York;* that was such an easy click, sent with a finality that I'd hoped would put my dilemma to rest. But it didn't (not even close). And so that obsession drives part of *HH*'s narrative, as Knapp's obsession with alcohol drives hers.

In one of my craft classes in my MFA program, we focused on stealing a trick here, another trick there from the writers we studied. From Paul Auster's *The Invention of Solitude*, I borrowed his technique of writing lists. From Jamaica Kincaid's *My Brother*, I copied her use of long, digressive sentences.

Perhaps I should buy a book on moving, copy the way others do it.

BEING ORDINARY

This morning, I awoke to turn on the computer, check emails—personal and business—went outside for a walk, returned—more email. I was undoubtedly a more prolific writer in pre-Internet days.

Email seems like a time thief, and therefore, bad. But it's also about connection, and that is good. My solitary life as a writer can't thrive without the outside world. In fact, writing is all about connection, even for work I don't publish. The manuscripts that live in my closet explore themes that caused me pain: *Knitting Lessons* is all about my longing for a baby. Guilt for wanting a life separate from my parents is in almost everything I write. By connecting to my brain and my heart, I was able to live with myself.

Those who know much more about yoga than I, say yoga, too, is about connection—to oneself and to the world. Perhaps that's why writing and yoga intertwine in my life. They each enable me to move past my failings. One way in particular that yoga serves me is through the concept of pausing. In *Bringing Yoga to Life*, Donna Farhi writes about how useful it is to do nothing (more "non-doing") when the urge to react is strong. Each time I remember that, I preempt a crisis.

I want to soak up every word of Farhi's book and take them further. I imagine myself as a yoga teacher, even though it feels late in life to pursue that discipline. When I tell my friends about my interest in the yoga teacher training, I add, *I'd never actually teach.*

I used to think that yoga and meditation were about being on a higher plane than the rest of us. I thought that a person who stood on his or her head and meditated (not necessarily at the same time) had sacred knowledge. They didn't live in a crowded city in a crowded apartment building, doing their laundry on Saturday mornings and pushing a shopping cart through the local grocery. I also thought writers—my God, writers!—were too esteemed to brush shoulders with me. I could never walk among them.

Then I became a writer and much later, a yogi. Both practices have helped me be ordinary. Today—so much to do. Grade papers, prepare lessons, come up with a plan for finding an apartment. (I'm not sure if Googling apartments in Prescott, Arizona, where a friend lives, counts.) If I'm lucky, I'll find more time to write, go to yoga, push the shopping cart.

How Students Learn

Yesterday I had a wonderful teaching moment. My class was discussing Edgar Allan Poe's "The Tell-Tale Heart," a story about a madman plotting to murder someone whose "vulture eye" drives him crazy. A student who was visibly repulsed asked, "Why would someone write this? What is the point?" I was about to launch into a dialogue about symbolism, when an idea intercepted.

"Let's write our own horror story," I said, "and see if we can figure it out." One student groaned, and I wondered if this was too immature an assignment for college freshmen. But I persevered. I suggested a few "ingredients" for the story: an abandoned church, a one-eyed cat, a wheelchair, and set the story at midnight. Then we went to work. The few times I looked up, I saw chairs faced sideways, notebooks on laps, heads down, hands moving fast, turning pages.

Most of the time, college students don't get class time to write just for writing's sake. They don't get to loosen up with a pen in hand (real pen, no keyboard) and an unusual assignment in a reading course. It may seem as if there's no real learning going on. But any time a class of freshmen writes—and then reads and listens to one another's work—there's learning.

I'm curious to see what the student who was repulsed comes back with after the weekend. I'm curious to see if "just for the fun of it" was a good enough reason to write a horror story.

THE PRESENT MOMENT

This morning, I walked toward school thinking about the concept of "the present moment." Which means that I wasn't actually in the present moment. I was having an imaginary conversation with an important person in my life about yoga.

I explained (in my imagining) how yoga's ultimate destination goes beyond therapy. At least to me, therapy's goal is to learn to cope well. What I gather from the texts I'm reading is that the goal of yoga is the absence of pain and suffering.

My important person asks (I'm still imagining), *How does one achieve absence from pain and suffering?* Feeling rather smug, I respond, *By returning to the present moment.* And he asks, *How?* I say, smugly, *By returning to the breath.*

By this point in our imaginary conversation, I had reached the door of the faculty room. I took out my ID card to unlock the door. But it was my Metrocard I tried passing through the buzzer. *So much for the present moment*, I thought, until I realized that my "mistake" was exactly right. I was in transit. From thinking and imaginary-conversationalist self to teacher- self.

And as teacher-self, I realized my response to *How does one achieve absence from pain and suffering?* was trite. What if one's present moment *is* pain and suffering? Concentration camp inmates and African-American slaves dissociated from their present moments to survive. I imagine my mother traveled to her childhood home, to the time when her mother was alive. What joy that would have been for my mother. "Momma loved me the best," she often said. It would be years later when my mother was safe in Brooklyn that she would stare into the horror.

Would it ultimately have been better for her if had she stared her situation down, one present moment at a time? Would she *not* have faced the monster later? Or, perhaps she did face him down—then and later.

My teacher-self forces me awake to the rote answers I give my ordinary self. And my teacher-self tells me there is so much I will never know.

Movie Day

After a semester of breaking down the elements of character and watching our flawed protagonists inch toward a goal, we watch the drama unfold before us.

Niki Caro's *Whale Rider* is one of my favorite movies to show students. The story of the Maori people in New Zealand living according to their ancestral traditions shows the conflicts that arise when a family member resists change. At the end of class, a student who had rarely spoken to me effusively thanked me for the great class. Another told me I'm a wonderful teacher. I was thrilled that my students' attention had been captured. Although it had little to do with me and everything to do with the movie's heroine, Paikea, and her grandfather, Koro.

I haven't felt this semester that I've given this class my best. Thoughts—and perhaps, anxiety—about where to move distracted me. My usual syllabus for this fiction class includes at least ten short stories, ending with Franz Kafka's *The Metamorphosis*. While there are always a few who question some of the stories' bizarre themes (such as in *The Metamorphosis*, when Gregor Samsa awakes as a bug), asking, "Why do we have to read this?" most enjoy the escape into literature. But I digress. *Whale Rider.*

I'm less inclined to think my students thanked me for my wonderful teaching skill than for the heightened experience of immersion in the present moment. No texting, emailing, or tuning out. Just a great story to get lost in.

A Wandering Jew

" **D**iscovering the Virtues of a Wandering Mind," by John Tierney in the *New York Times* talks about the positive side of zoning out. It's also wreaking havoc with my present-moment practice. If a "wandering mind" is a good way to cultivate ideas, then is being in the present moment overrated?

What is my present moment? Is it a void I'm afraid of looking into? Or an embarrassment of riches I can't choose from? I did say yes to moving out of Brooklyn (never mind the twenty-seven years).

There's a fiction contest I want to enter with a story I wrote a few years ago. There's the "Why I Write" essay for *Poets & Writers*. There's *HH* still in revision. And there are the places I can move to.

And, too, there are bows. Silk, tulle, velvet, organza. When I get into the glitter and sparkle and fun of it, bows take up my apartment; fabrics spill all over the floor, old-fashioned buttons and silver snaps dot the sofa, invisible thread—well, that is its own challenge.

I put a red and black bow in my hair one morning. I wore it into the upscale department store Henri Bendel's. A young saleswoman asked me where I bought it. I smiled and took my credit! I love the immersion in folding, crunching, pouffing, wrapping, sewing, gluing, inventing.

I took out all the stuff later and made a bow just for the sake of it. I began thinking of getting enough bows made this summer to take them to Bendel's for their Open See. It's a day when they open their doors to anyone with a product. I want that feeling of adventure—showing up on line in the early morning hours, calling myself a designer, for the day.

My present moment is a cornucopia of color and ideas. But I need to write that essay, enter the contest, find a place to move to . . . I can't access my writing self with all that color and texture at my elbow.

My mind wanders. It floods itself and drowns in ideas. Consciously, I'm trying to have good present moments. Unconsciously, I can't be certain.

AWAY

I visited a friend on Fire Island for a few days, minus my laptop. I didn't miss my computer until uneasy moments of displacement swept over me. Normally at such times, I'd set out for a café, set up a little office, and, in front of the keyboard, I'd remember who I am. And so I had to face the challenge of remembering me, away from my comfort zone.

Just before heading for the Long Island Railroad and my Fire Island escape, I was in anxiety mode. I had to make a stop at school, take care of paperwork, then rush in the sweltering heat, carrying stuff (although *not* said computer) to make the train on time. I had a flash of looking ahead longingly to my return home—laundry done, me showered and relaxed.

I hadn't even left Manhattan, and coming home felt so good. But when I allowed the comfort of my friend's cottage to take me over, I was glad to be away, caught up in the moment. That is, until we headed for the beach—umbrellas, chairs, towels, so much fuss—and I thought longingly of the shower I'd have when we got back, the pleasure of washing off the paste of suntan lotion and sand.

The ocean was soothing, spectacular. We dug our chairs into the sand, hammered in the umbrella, sat back, relaxed. At the ocean's edge, the cool water ran between my toes. The present moment came to me in the crush of a wave. Wishing away time isn't always about wanting to go from something bad to better. It's unknown territory that scares me. If I'm okay here, why go there? Kabat-Zinn might respond, *If you're okay here, you'll be okay there.*

How simple and true, and yet how very complicated. In that complication, "okay" can be so easily lost, wished away without even realizing. Today, back home and at the computer, I write my life, aware that if I'm not very careful, I can write away my life.

READING TO MY FATHER

L ast night I began reading *The Book of Lights*, by Chaim Potok. This story of a rabbinical student enthralled by the Kaballah took me to my father's bedside. I imagined him as he was at the end of his life. I sit beside him (in this imagining), reading aloud.

When God decided to create the world, He first produced a flame of a scintillating lamp . . .

My father presses my palm and smiles; he loves the sounds of the Orthodox world these words create. And how appreciated I feel, bringing this joy to him, giving my father an end to his life that is a perfect circle. For he was born into the world of Orthodoxy. And it is this world I battled against as a young girl in my efforts to be American. When my father spoke Yiddish on our Brooklyn streets, I turned my face, as if I didn't know him; when he went to shul on Shabbos, carrying his siddur and talis, I pretended he was like the American fathers on television, going to work.

In keeping with the complicated ironies of my life, it is my father's home I now often wish to discover. *Tell me about the Talmud*, I insist to my father in this bedside fantasy. *And Kaballah! Explain this, too*. My father pats my hand and smiles. His stroke has rendered him speechless. But for us, understanding has always been on a cellular level.

My father's love, a wrenching and gorgeous miracle.

E arly at Starbucks this morning, I ran into a neighbor. We chatted about my upcoming (and amorphous) move, former employers and Emerson (of all things). After that, I met another neighbor, more chatting—complex early morning stuff, most likely the remnants of REM sleep. And in the midst of all this brainy conversing, a voice inside said I must get home and write my father—not a letter, but write him alive.

My father was born in 1915. The distance between his village and my mother's was an hour by carriage. In fact, the possibility of my parents' meeting in Europe, had there not been a Hitler, would have been entirely possible.

As a young man, my father worked in Muncash at two jobs: he was a grocery distributor and a window dresser. My favorite detail of his life as a young man was how he enjoyed visiting Muncash before the war, a city hectic with cafés and young people laughing and dancing.

When I close my eyes I see my father as a dashing young man, with his high, aristocratic forehead, his longish nose, his avocado eyes.

I wish I could choose a moment of the past and freeze-frame it, like a photograph. I would insert myself into a time machine and travel back to 1939 when my father was twenty-four. I would sit across the marble table from him in Muncash, sipping an espresso. I would ask a stranger to snap our picture; I would seal it in my mind's eye.

I would wonder if my father recognized my own avocado eyes.

W hen I think of my father, my brain settles, my breath slows, a certain kind of peace descends.

Many years ago, Chaim Potok was among my favorite writers. But I feared reading him when his words took me to a sorrowful, lonely place. The book was *Davita's Harp,* a coming-of-age novel of a young Jewish girl who yearned to connect with the religion her parents rejected. The book took me deep inside myself even though that wasn't my story, not on the surface at least.

That day so many years ago, when my swing went level to the bar, terror and guilt froze in time. My father was inches away, yet lost in a distant loneliness.

There, in the pit of me, is the door to my father's home, the door I wish to knock on.

ON TO CRAIGSLIST

I went on Craigslist to look at apartment rentals. There are brokered apartments for a fee and no fee. The assumption might be that paying a fee will produce a better apartment, but that's not necessarily true. The studio I now live in had no fee. Should I end up in Philadelphia (it's possible . . .), the landlord will pay. That's how many cities out of New York work.

I have an appointment to see three apartments in Queens: two in Rego Park, one in Forest Hills. The appeal: more space, lower rent. The non-appeal: I know only one person in Queens.

My fall semester starts up today. After class I'll take the F train and see the broker-no-fee-apartments.

FINISHING SOMETHING

I scrolled through the website www.shewrites.com and read an interesting blog post by novelist Kamy Wicoff. She discusses the difference between blogging and writing. I like the way she lays out how writing—as opposed to blogging—requires time, nurturance, lots of thought, and did I say, time? I'm living in this distinction these days, alternately blogging and working on the "Why I Write" essay.

One of the pleasures of blogging is the immediate gratification. Regardless of how productive (or not) my day is, when I write a blog entry, I put thought into my words, in a way that offers some sort of insight. (At least, that is my goal.) That my words get read is an extra bonus—even if my "stats" reveal an audience of two.

But my blog entries are static; I don't save them as drafts and look at them in a day or two before making them LIVE. I don't push myself to hit lyrical notes while also searching for greater meaning. When writing essays, and especially when revising them, I push and probe my first responses. Essayist Phillip Lopate calls this process "doubting oneself on the page."

Ah yes . . . the "Why I Write" essay. I've never been good at writing an essay on a given topic. But I have an introduction I like:

I hadn't planned on becoming a writer. When I did, there was something naïve and wonderful about discovering I could put words together in a way that lit me up—and I would discover—others wanted to read. I was forty-four then—no stranger to searching for some form of creative expression to satisfy a deep need to prove myself.

I read Daphne Merkin's brilliant essay "My Life in Therapy" in the *New York Times Magazine.* I couldn't help comparing her slogging through one therapist after the other for forty years as similar to my memoir compulsion.

Maybe I'll start a futuristic story, set in a time when memory is passé. All past experience is collectively stored on a computer chip. Then . . . stolen! Yes, by one poor human who carries the memories of the world—and that person is *not* in any way me.

GAINING FOCUS?

"Why I Write" is in the mail! It felt good to tick one thing off my to-do writing list. Sending out work makes me feel productive as a writer. Publishing the long-suffering *HH* feels less important.

So . . . apartments in Queens. The no-fee-broker apartments were highly livable—with more space than I now have and small, separate kitchens. One had an eat-in kitchen! But I can't see myself in these family-centered neighborhoods that are quiet and away from everyone.

Yes . . . I'm aware Iowa City Tucson Albuquerque are even farther, quieter, and likely family centered as well. But, somehow, they aren't comparable.

Writing Whores

I had a writing friend who said that writers are whores. She meant that we take whatever is happening in our lives—or in the lives of others—and spin it for a paycheck. I took her words personally at the time as I often wrote about my parents, and many of my essays were published. I remember putting my fingers to my cheek, as if to comfort the place I'd been slapped for my whorish ways.

There are so many motivations to tell personal stories; each writer (and storyteller) has their own. A few I can think of are the release of a burden, to inform and help others, to make sense of a life, and, for me—because I simply cannot *not* write. My fingers move through my sleep and tap Morse code upon my dreams; stories beg for release . . . in particular this one, that my life still spins on:

One day when I was fourteen, my mother took to her bed believing she was dying of heart failure. It was shortly after we'd moved from Crown Heights to Flatlands. She couldn't go on living, she said. The doctor was on his way.

My mother had been so happy about the move. Flatlands had lawns and driveways and screen doors that snapped closed; it was my favorite sound in the world.

My mother had believed life there would be as it appeared for the people on the television shows we had watched. In December Bride, the woman of the house leaned over her white fence talking to her neighbors. She wanted to be a December Bride, too. Our Formica kitchen, self-defrost refrigerator, pink-tiled bathroom were symbols of modern America—the world my mother had pictured an ocean ago.

Yet, there we were in the carpeted living room, looking out onto low-level houses, manicured lawns, and my mother was flirting with dying.

I think my mother needed to die so she could be reborn.

On that long-ago day when she took to her bed, saying she had heart failure, the doctor came to our apartment, holding his black doctor's bag. He put the stethoscope to her chest and listened. Then there was a whisper, a low of hum of words I couldn't decipher. Later, he stood before me in the living room. He said she wasn't dying. She had anxiety.

My mother called me to her bedside. "Simala, come here."

I sat on the side of the bed next to her. She sat up, leaned against the headboard. Her skin was moist, always so moist—from Nivea and something else that seeped through her pores so that she shone.

I held her hand. "Mom, you're beautiful. I love you so much."

"Don't worry, Simala. A young girl needs her mother. For you, I'm going to live."

The crush of my mother's life bearing down on me. The responsibility in my young hands. The relief, too. To know that I could save her.

⁓

Where would I be without writing mentors who gave me permission to write my life? Kim Chernin's *In My Mother's House* mirrored my conflicts with a mother who'd lived a life far worthier than mine of being written. Helen Epstein's groundbreaking *Children of the Holocaust* was the first of its kind about the sons and daughters of survivors. I recall my relief in learning of other mothers like mine whose traumas were in their children's hands.

Vivian Gornick's *Fierce Attachments* gave me insight into my own "fierce attachment." Amy Tan's *The Joy Luck Club* revealed that my peers, regardless of ethnicity, had this difficult yet nurturing bond.

Where would I be without my role models? Are they whores? More like my saviors, every one.

A HOLIDATE

Today, Yom Kippur, I have a date with my mother. I'll meet her in the pews at the synagogue where I'll say Yizkor. My grief will meet me too, for it arises during prayer as if it's our first time together.

As awful as grief is, there's something alive and free about crying fresh, hard tears. I remember when my father passed away, a friend told me, "Enjoy your grief." I understood immediately: one day the pain would lift, and with that relief, my connection to my father would fade. Today, I'm not sad, although I have a distinct wish to recapture a Yom Kippur past, in fact a very specific ritual. After the shofar was blown, signifying the end of the twenty-four-hour fast, my mother and I raced home from shul. As we ran, my mother lit the cigarette hidden in her glove. At home, we prepared the table with delectable foods. We licked the salt off our fingers from the Nova Scotia lox, the white fish that fell out of its ripply golden skin.

I miss running home with my mother, waving to my father across the pews, gathering with my girlfriends in front of a synagogue to look for boys.

I miss not knowing what the future will hold.

WHERE TO GO

This morning I searched on the Internet for apartments in Ocean Grove, my favorite place on the Jersey Shore. This beach town, a two-hour drive from Manhattan, is a city girl's mecca, for it is one square mile, with a Main Street filled with cafés and trendy clothing stores.

I made two phone calls and set up appointments: one is for a nine-month house rental, the other an apartment on the first floor of a house. I felt excited and renewed, filled with hope like when I sent those grad-school applications into the world.

Afterwards, while walking to Starbucks, contemplating the long and expensive commute, these words flew into my brain: *It's not so much where I live, but how I live.* Then I had a revelation about Manhattan: the thing that keeps me rooted here is that I never have to send the city an email, asking, *Are you available?* Fourteen floors below my window, the city beckons, *Come on down!*

And so I do—to Starbucks, the twenty-four-hour hardware store, CVS (twenty-four-hour too), or to simply walk up or down Second Avenue. I walk and browse and think.

A positive experience in my MFA program happened in my poetry class, when I met a fellow writer born in Brooklyn and yearning for Manhattan. Walt Whitman nudged himself next to me in my class on, well . . . Walt Whitman!

My Manhatoe, he wrote, longing for the place he left to nurse soldiers during the Civil War. When he returned to Manhattan from the South he was broken by sickness, no longer the carefree man on the cover of *Leaves of Grass*. His sense of place had been reshaped by war.

My parents' Holocaust experiences had shaped my sense of place. But unlike Whitman, I was born into war's aftereffects; I had no prewar place to yearn for, not my own anyway. There was my mother's home that she longed for, her entire American life. Her village was sealed in memory, unchanged and perfect; but in real life, tarnished and broken.

My yearning for a place that doesn't exist is as present as my breath.

LIFE IN REVISION

P *oets & Writers* rejected my "Why I Write." I was disappointed . . .
in fact, surprised. I thought my essay was perfect (always a red
flag). When I returned to it, I found points where I could take the work
deeper, in particular, uncovering the driving force of what brings me
to the page. I discovered that having been a secretarial major with low
self-esteem and aspirations infuses me now with the need to use my
intellect.

I revised and sent the essay off to the op-ed editor of the *Philadelphia
Inquirer*. Op-ed pages have been good homes for my work, the *Philly
Inquirer*, very much so. They published one of my first essays, "Pondering
the Biological Clock's Tick," after it had been rejected by other publications. Often getting published is all about finding the right home.

I returned to old work this week, reassembled, refreshed, revised. I
felt productive doing the thing I often feel I was put on this earth for—
to observe and write it all down.

Early Morning Thoughts on Memoir

My literature class this semester is absorbed by Hosseini's novels. We read *The Kite Runner* and then moved on to his follow-up, *A Thousand Splendid Suns*. This book, also set in Afghanistan, follows the lives of two women—one traditional, one modern—living under Taliban rule. In keeping with the theme of Afghanistan, we're now reading *Kabul Beauty School*, a memoir by Deborah Rodriquez. I've been enjoying this book about an American woman who was part of a beauty-school venture in Afghanistan. I've been imagining myself going off to a country in need, providing some worthy assistance—finding a purpose in helping others find theirs.

But this morning I tooled around on Google. I discovered there's backlash to Rodriquez's book. Even though characters portrayed in the book were anonymous, Kabul women who studied at her school and befriended her are in danger. In the book's opening scene, a young Afghan woman is terrified. She's about to marry a man her parents chose, and she's not a virgin. Tradition calls for the presentation of a white hanky with the bride's virgin blood to be displayed after the couple's first night. Rodriquez helps her friend fake a bloody hanky. The scene is informative and amusing and it's a grabber. It's also now the source of anxiety for many Afghan women, who fear being discovered of not having been virgin brides.

As the story moves on and reveals why the author is there, the true memoir unfolds. It's Rodriquez's funny and heartfelt story of finding a purpose in teaching women a marketable skill. She isn't an MD, RN, or social worker; her cosmetology license is her prized commodity. She, not the women, is the heart of the book. But publishers of memoir today look for a story with an opening that shocks or assures readers of lots of conflict to come. Rodriquez had much conflict in her own life—an abusive marriage, single parenthood. In fact she writes, in comparison: ". . . [Afghanistan] felt like paradise."

I can think of many peak moments in my life when everything changed—certainly the day my mother said she was dying. Were she still alive, I would likely not have written about that time. My need to protect her was immense.

When I did finally open up to her, I chose the worst time. My mother really was dying; I needed to be upbeat, to call her and tell her, "Everything is fine." I'd just had a devastating breakup, and in my grief thought my mother and I deserved a chance to be real.

And so I called her. It was a Sunday, 5:00 p.m.

"Hi, Mom, how are you?"

"I'm not so good, Símala. I'm going to sleep." Her voice was barely audible.

"Okay. Feel better," I said, noting that she went to bed earlier each time we spoke.

"Are you okay?" she whispered.

"I'm sad. I had a breakup."

"I'm sorry," she said, then drifted away, and we said our good-byes. I hated myself for bringing my misery to her; what had I been thinking?

One minute later I called back. "Mom, I didn't mean to tell you that. I'm fine, it was nothing. I don't know why I said that."

"Good, sweetheart, I was upset."

"No. Don't be. You know how I am; I say things I don't mean."

A glimmer of a voice. "Okay. Thank you for calling."

We never spoke again.

I need to write of happier times so I can remember and hold them; that's where the joy is. That's where I'm uplifted into something greater than some of my worst present moments. Common memoir lore is that one must go into the dark places, deep inside those peak moments.

But I've already been in those closets, rummaged through those drawers. Lately, I'm more intrigued by surfaces, what gets wiped away and what remains.

END OF SEMESTER

The end of semester is a time to reevaluate. An entire plot summary of a movie taken from Amazon.com, was explained as a way to merely set the stage for the essay to follow. A movie review taken from Facebook: *It's just a small amount, and you said if we didn't use research we'd get a D.* And the most frequent: *I only forgot to add the quotation marks.* Then there are the relatives who died to explain massive absences. And the forthright begs: *I have to pass this class!* However, when given the opportunity to make up missing work, some don't take it and expect a good grade, anyway.

U.S. educators are taking a thrashing these days. Teachers are getting called out for passing unprepared students to the next grade. What I'm wondering is, when do students take responsibility? They're eighteen and older. Why do they come to college expecting to get away with bad behavior?

Great teachers can become terrible teachers when students with no respect for boundaries pounce. When an administrator says to treat each student the same—that's not as simple as it sounds. Many students receiving financial aid need to get a minimum grade of a B in each class. Students earning a C and lower come up with all sorts of pleas. One of these students cried when I told him he was getting C+. He said he was homeless and the school was helping him get housing. Classes had ended. Grades were due. He had five days to make up five homework assignments. He did them. He got his B.

In between all this mental chatter today, I'm thinking again about living on the beach, even though I'm not a beach girl; I'm drawn to the country, mountains, trees. I'm thinking too about bows and that I should take out the red velvet, the black tulle and make something.

Finding the Right Project

I didn't go to Ocean Grove. The bus ride that I usually love appeared in my mind as a ride to lonelyville. What would I do once I settled into my little house? Yes, there is yoga, and spirituality with a capital *S*, as Ocean Grove is a dry town; many twelve-steppers live there.

I trusted my feelings, not always the best method for plotting my life. But when I awoke, the plan to make the 10:00 a.m. bus seemed wrong—and so I cancelled. Then I resurrected my dead novel, *Knitting Lessons*, decreed as such several years ago. As I read through the book, I wasn't at all aware of the distraction I kicked up.

I moved chapters around, changed third person to first, "is" to "was," and entered the world of Suzannah and Larry, a couple trying unsuccessfully for two years to have a baby. Then Larry has an affair; the woman gets pregnant, and Suzannah . . . well, at that point the line between her and me begins to blur.

I felt Suzannah's longing to have a child with Larry and then her pain that another woman carries his child. I felt, too, the loss of Suzannah's Grandma Bella, a Holocaust survivor who had taught Suzannah to knit, as my mother had taught me. But after two days I realized that the project no longer felt right. The autobiographical element that had worked its way into the book was not me anymore. Larry had been chiseled from the memory of a man I'd been involved with. I had poured all my sadness about our breakup into Suzannah's heart.

And Grandma Bella, modeled after my mother, was no longer a character I could bring fully to life. Developing the story, once therapeutic and fun, felt like a step back to something that had worked itself out off the page.

I put the pages away, filed away all the CDs (circa late 1990s) with the manuscript saved in umpteen versions. Having my writing life based in reality, as opposed to the fantasy of how I'd like it to be, is akin to a good yoga class.

FYI 1, the thing about moving out of the city is that it feels like a fresh start. I picture myself as someone different, without a back story.

FYI 2, I'm still thinking of taking the yoga teacher training. And this provides me with a whole bunch of new places to Google.

Making Lemonade

I'm working on an essay, "The Ambivalent Memoirist." Instead of whining about my difficulties with the demon *HH,* I took my dilemma to the page.

After trying unsuccessfully for several years to complete a memoir, I enrolled in an MFA program. I was hopeful the enforced deadlines and the required graduation thesis would push me through my anxieties. After one year in the memoir writing program, my work wasn't going well.

Wanting to write a memoir and writing one to bring to class for feedback were infinitely different endeavors. Not only were manuscripts critiqued, but so too were the family conflicts we brought to the page. My classmates wrote about their siblings' addictions, childhood molestations, a parent in prison, every version of childhood neglect. They brought to class dramatic, wrenching (and depressing) manuscripts. I had my own burden of writing material. . .

The trickiest part of writing this essay is that the subject matter veers in many directions. While writing about my ambivalence about memoir—more precisely, my discomfort revealing family intimacies—my MFA unhappiness creeps in.

What I want to say about writing programs is that they all have their own personality; one way they're similar is that ultimately you put your work into the hands of ten (and maybe more) others for critique. You can't control what they say. In one of my classes, students critiqued manuscripts and also the lives we wrote about. That was tough.

At their best, MFA programs inspire endless writing due to deadlines and peers you connect with. I had one friend in my class; her feedback and support helped me continue in the program.

My aborted dreams of Iowa Tucson Albuquerque hadn't helped me to accept a so-so program, also known as Plan B. The problem with having a "safe" Plan B is that just by having it, it can become Plan A.

Ah yes ... "The Ambivalent Memoirist." It feels good to make something of my years of work.

I wanted to get it all on the page, free myself of a lifetime grip my parents had on me. But I could not reveal intimacies that might cause my parents pain or embarrassment. My feelings for them were a complicated mix of love and pity. That was a problem; I needed a ninety-page thesis to graduate. My mentor suggested I focus the book on my mother, because she was no longer alive.

It is not always easier to write about a parent when they are dead. For me, the possibility of breaking through my fears and my mother reading my words no longer exists. That knowledge leaves a terrible emptiness.

I'm amazed that memoirs actually get finished.

YEARNING

My friend Diane is moving to Tbilisi, Georgia. Just like that, she got a job and is packing up herself and her five-year-old, Jill, and heading to a New Job and New Life. I envy her ability to thoroughly engage in the world, even when that world is thousands (and more thousands) of miles away. How great it must feel to say yes to an exotic life.

Until two weeks ago, the only Georgia I knew of was in the U.S. Then I did a Google search. The ancient city with its mountain views made my heart sing. I'm losing a friend and her gorgeous daughter, although Diane disagrees. *You can get a job there and teach English.* She says this so casually, as if moving across the globe is a walk around the block. As if she isn't talking to *me*.

FYI, According to Holy Google, there is yoga in Tbilisi.

EXORCISING GHOSTS

I n the mid-1980s, I went to Kripalu, a yoga education center in the Berkshires in western Massachusetts, which was then an ashram. I wasn't particularly interested in yoga or Eastern religions. A friend who lived in the area (and as it turned out, knew little about Kripalu) thought I'd like it and so I went.

The austerity and silence were eerie. I slept in a dorm, a room with painted stone walls and rows of beds. Around that time I had just begun opening the door to my parents' Holocaust experiences. Lying on my narrow bed, I felt as though I were in Auschwitz. I cut my visit short and ran, as I have from many places that brought that harrowing world to me.

This past weekend I returned to the "scene of the crime." I needed a vacation and am now open to yoga and Eastern philosophies. In a workshop there, I learned *ahimsa*—the yogic principle of nonviolence, or not causing harm. I practiced *ahimsa* when a woman talked about how proud she is for her contributions to technology. I was tempted to say technology and texting make me crazy. But I paused.

I had a good weekend. I enjoyed the choice of three levels of yoga classes. I took beginner, which were slow and playful, without the strict adherence to alignment like at my at-home studio. I liked that it was a half hour before we roused ourselves for a downward-facing dog.

I slept in a private room, not the dorm. For a few minutes, the white brick wall felt prison-like and creepy. I told myself, *It's okay to be here*; the feeling passed, as a feeling often does when I permit myself to be where I am and with whatever or whoever.

I wondered about taking their yoga teacher training. The in-residence cost is about $5,000 plus, depending on accommodations. Then, of course, I'd have to figure out a way to do it and still earn a living.

I returned home, feeling content. I didn't go to Kripalu to scare away old demons. But, in some way, I think I did.

All Over the Place

While I tried to meditate this morning, many thoughts collided. *Should I take the yoga teacher training? Yes. At my current yoga studio or maybe Kripalu? What if I move to Philly?* Mindfulness meditation, which is what I'm striving for, doesn't ask me to stop my thoughts. It only asks that I notice them.

But when one preoccupation freezes in my brain, sitting still is excruciating. My impulse is to get up and do something. Make that phone call to my cousin Joan who lives near Philly and tell her, *I will move to Philadelphia! Let's look at apartments.* (I'm supposed to let this thought go by, like all thoughts.)

I'm reminded why I write in a sometimes addictive way; emptying my mind on paper stops my thoughts from paralyzing me. But today, writing about my feelings isn't what I want to do. Escaping into something not about me feels healthier.

My memoir may never be published, but it's had a small audience by virtue of my MFA peers and friends who read sections. Maybe that's enough.

Now, this moment, perhaps I find my peace while conjuring places to move to, and then not going to them.

Interpreting Heroes

Two of my English classes are reading John Updike's short story "A & P." This story, about a young man who impulsively quits his job as a cashier, separates my classes into two groups. There are those who go with the interpretation that Sammy was courageous for quitting a job he hated, even though he didn't have another waiting. And there are just as many who see Sammy as a fool.

The reading and analysis of this story always reminds me how difficult objectivity is. As the teacher, my job is to provide an atmosphere for students to freely engage in discussion. But, my own value system often creeps in. In Updike's story, the A & P symbolizes the 1950s culture in which Sammy lives. Housewives ("houseslaves in pin curlers") push their carts up and down the aisles, while bored Sammy ogles "these three girls in bathing suits" who enter the store, representing rebellion and sexuality.

I love the interpretation that the girls are a metaphor for the freedom Sammy craves. When my students wander in this direction, I feel I've done my job well. But then just as quickly, a student will counter, "Only an irresponsible person would quit without another paycheck to count on." I'm reminded that a job of any kind can be a ticket to freedom. My students are working class, and many are the first in their family to attend college.

I wonder if I'm pushing an interpretation, when that isn't my job. And isn't interpretation open to interpretation?

TEACHING GRAMMAR

E ach composition professor brings his or her own strengths to the
classroom. This is what I tell my students when one or two (or
God help me . . . more) say, "That's not how I learned it last semester." I
don't want to criticize another teacher, nor do I want to reveal the gaps
in my English education. But with a degree in writing—not a PhD in
English—grammar is not my favorite subject to teach.

I learned everything I know about grammar in my secretarial classes. My Pitman shorthand teacher taught me the comma-by-instinct
methodology, and I never learned the rules. Therein lies my challenge
when I teach grammar; students want words like superlatives, claus-
es, modifiers, dangling thises and thats. I ask them to read their work
aloud and listen to the natural pauses—even though I know grammar
isn't that simple. I also send them to the tutoring center so they can
get the formula, the subject/verb answer. The problem is, it's so easily
forgotten.

Last week, while working on the notorious run-on sentence, a student had trouble understanding the difference between a comma and
a period. I was at a loss. His confusion stayed with me for days. So, too,
did the question "When using a book for research, how do we know

where to find the right information?" I was startled. I mentioned the table of contents, the index. What is Google doing to students?

To talk about freshmen students being unprepared for college work is now a cliché. How can we teach them what they need to know? I have a handful of students who belong in honors classes in better colleges, but they can't afford them. I have other students who write at eighth-grade level, were placed in remedial writing, and, after several tries, passed the test to get into freshman English. They still struggle. Saying students are unprepared doesn't get us anywhere. Where do we go from there?

MOVING

I called my cousin Joan last night. She said she'll pick me up at the bus station in Center City, Pennsylvania. That might be the perfect spot for me—Brooklyn Heights-ish, with great culture, restaurants, and high on the walkability scale.

But after a night's sleep, my first thought is, *What was this home girl thinking?* I love concocting plans about where I'll live—how I'll commute to my New York work life, and then rush back home to a place where four hundred square feet is affordable. But in the early morning hours, these plans feel as though they're someone else's.

Which leads me to the questions: Does my anxiety tell me going to Philly is the wrong move? Some might say I'm nervous about change.

How do I know the difference between anxiety and a bad idea?

Sometimes I erect very high fences, when it's completely unnecessary.

STILL SEARCHING

A las. Today I'll go back to Queens, which has always been an un-familiar borough to me. The neighborhoods: Astoria, Sunnyside, Long Island City. Next weekend: Nyack, an artsy town with spectacular views of the Hudson.

A TEACHER'S LAMENT

In one-to-one conferences today about papers, a student questioned my accuracy about punctuation—not a bad thing to do, except his higher source was the squiggly line in the Microsoft Word document. We bantered for at least five minutes. Feeding the squiggle (herein known as the MS Monster) any form of punctuation—comma, semicolon, colon (doesn't seem to matter)—makes the MS Monster go away. And so, instead of having a lesson on complete sentences, we (actually, he) pondered, could MS Word be wrong?

Then there was the student working on a research paper. He put into quotations what he wrote in his own words, not the material taken word for word from another source. In an odd logic, what he did made sense. Writing is talking, only it's on the page. One's own words . . . "talk talk talk."

Then there was the "conversation" with my Chair. Which led to a *one-dollar-an-hour raise*. Arghh . . . I need a new career.

Last night I attended an open house at the studio where I practice yoga, for information on the teacher training. They opened with a half-hour practice, then described the program: posture and alignment, anatomy, meditation, reading, and discussion of sacred texts and books by important yoga people like B. K. S. Iyengar and Donna Farhi.

Is this what I really want to do? The price tag is steep, about $3,500, plus reading materials. My gut doesn't know . . . is this possible? Don't we always get a sign somewhere inside of us, which we may or may not listen to?

Monday night I baked applesauce muffins—I love baking. I have so many essay ideas; sentences eject themselves from my brain with nowhere to land. One of these days, very soon, I'll trash *HH* and start something new.

In Movement

By the time I had left Brooklyn in 2004, I had walked the Brooklyn Bridge, which was visible from my bedroom window, over two thousand times. I loved that one-mile walk that stretched across the East River like a tightrope. While walking toward Manhattan I came alive. Often I kept on walking through City Hall, then Chinatown, Soho, the East Village, and all the way up to Bloomingdales on 60th and Lexington Avenue.

But no matter how far I walked, at some point there was the turning around and running down subway steps to go home to Brooklyn. And with that pivot, there was a feeling of want thumping in my chest, a feeling that I wasn't going where I wanted to go.

Now, I'm here, in Manhattan; I can look for a job outside the city and live wherever that will be. My friends tell me I'll still be me wherever I go. They say "searching" is part of my personality. So, too, is indecisiveness and saying no.

I hate these things about myself.

Jill and Diane are in Tbilisi; my neighbor is moving to Kenya next week. She doesn't know what to make of me when I tell her I was afraid to move to Iowa.

There are so many ways to live one's life. If I'm not careful I can spend mine waiting, not quite alive until I get to there.

My gut is still not talking to me.

Is the Process Enough?

A *New York Times* op-ed by Bob Herbert, "College the Easy Way," has been occupying my classes. Herbert maintains that students would rather party than study, and college administrators give them the okay by having low expectations. Many of my students agree. Those who do work hard resent those who don't yet come away with the same grades. I wish they could hold on to the fact that the learning, for its own sake, means a lot.

Last week I left a yoga class with numerous injuries. My wonderful philosophy about how props help me to be true to my own abilities? Gone. My no-comparing? Out the window. My knee and back pain were the result of competing with others (who didn't even notice me). Process was the last thing on my mind.

FYI 1, I didn't see any apartments in Sunnyside, Long Island City, and Astoria, but I did explore the neighborhoods. Sunnyside is pretty with gardens and trees, but no yoga. Astoria (the hip part) is very young. Long Island City is quiet. And out of my price range.

FYI 2, I didn't trash *HH*. I sent it to an editor for feedback and Help (capital *H*).

FYI 3, I had lunch with an acquaintance who lives in a rent-stabilized building in Manhattan. (Something to do with getting on a list.) I herewith admit to setting in motion, something I thought I would never do again—create a Plan B.

ENTITLEMENT

I love when a book I read for pleasure becomes a text I'll assign to my class. *Grace and Grit,* by Lilly Ledbetter, is her story of growing up in Alabama in the late 1940s and '50s in a poor, uneducated family. She went on to work in supervisory positions at Goodyear, where she was harassed and paid much less than her male counterparts.

What gripped me the most was Ledbetter's acceptance of jobs that I would never have considered. She worked twelve-hour days in factories and on production lines, had a stint at Tyson, where she slaughtered chickens, and never flinched from the physical abuses of her work. I've had numerous jobs that I disliked and felt demeaned by, even though I kept my hands clean, my clothes stylish, and a warm cup of coffee on my desk.

My expectation was that I would have a comfortable job. I didn't see it as an entitlement. Today, I wonder where such expectations come from. Is it the culture I was raised in? My assessment of the world and the place I assume for myself? Or is already decided by where my parents and their parents (and further back than that) began?

My father's first job in America was for a butcher, where he cut up chickens and beef. His father's job in Czechoslovakia was picking and crating ripe plums and selling them to grocers. Both of them had stained yet grateful hands. My clean hands were not always grateful.

Sense of It All

I went to a *kirtan* Saturday night—an evening of spiritual chanting—to hear Krishna Das, a guru in the world of devotional chanting. The candlelit room was filled with people of all ages seated on the floor and chairs, swaying and singing. The hippie-mood spiraled me back in time to the days of Woodstock.

It was 1969. At eighteen, I was all set to go to the concert, awaiting my pickup at 2:00 a.m. Then my brother telephoned from a phone off the New York State Thruway, where traffic was backed up for twenty miles. He painted a convincing portrait to my parents of why I should stay home. My 2:00 a.m. ride left without me and attended what turned out to be the event that defined a generation. Almost attending was the nonevent that defined me.

Mercifully, my friend Laurie hadn't gone to Woodstock either. We spent that eerie day together. The streets, normally filled with pedestrians and cars, were empty. It seemed as if there had been a nuclear fallout. Laurie and I wandered around Plum Beach—a deserted strip of sand and sea, somewhere near Sheepshead Bay—a place we were never able to find again. It was as if we had entered a Twilight Zone-ish sphere for two lonely teens who were the only ones left on earth.

Today I awoke to startling news: Osama bin Laden was killed. My reminiscence of all things Woodstock was eclipsed. But after the initial shock, my feelings about the news were blurry. Celebrating murdering someone seemed barbaric. Even though I remember as a child, having fantasies of torturing Adolph Eichmann when he was tried in 1961. The trial was televised, and I knew what he looked like. I lay awake at night and imagined him sitting in an electric chair, his straight black hair pasted to his forehead. I saw a line of all the Jews in the world pass in front of him; one would have the power to kill him, but Eichmann wouldn't know who.

When I went to work, I discovered my students' feelings about Osama bin Laden were blurry, too. Maybe they didn't want to say what I felt, that murder felt wrong. Some thought the story is a hoax; others talked of retaliation, and not with fear, but as if killing were a computer war game. One student is from Pakistan; he fears how he will now be looked at, here in New York. He's the only one whose feelings penetrated, reaching this thought I've been trying to repress. More violence.

None of this had yet happened when I sat in a room with Krishna Das. His voice, along with his awestruck audience, brought me to being eighteen years old and believing the world would give peace a chance.

Out of Hiding

I just sent an email to the editor at the *New York Times* who found my essay "Keeping Alive the Dreams of Love" before it hit the slush pile. It was 1996; I believed at that time, I'd be writing him much sooner about my writing success.

In my email to Wonderful Editor was a link to an unexpected and wonderful review of *On My Way to Someplace Else* on Jesse Kornbluth's website, www.headbutler.com.

Charm has become a high ideal for female writers these days — that is, for women who write the short sketch and the quirky op-ed . . . This is a shout-out for protein, served up by a writer you don't know in a book from a publisher you never heard of. "On My Way to Someplace Else" is short — just 113 pages — . . ."

Many years ago, when I sent that essay to the *Times*, I was experimenting and having fun with the discovery that I could write. I was like a child who had just learned to crawl. I wanted to go into every corner, every dark closet. Sometimes I wish I could stay there, in that wonderful discovery state.

The other day, my friend Gayle and I signed a contract. We each agreed to write a frivolous novel (as if it is as easy as that). The point: to take a break from the serious subject matter we usually delve into. But this venture will have to wait . . . Today, I bask in my "fame" and ponder the reviewer's words: "Adulthood seems to elude her."

FYI, "Why I Write" found a home in the *Philadelphia Inquirer.* This has re-stirred the move-to-Philadelphia cauldron.

SWITCHING GEARS

I received back my editor's critiqued copy of *Halfway Home*. She suggested I restructure, so that the story is told chronologically, or to use Creative (capital *C* on purpose) transitions. In other words, the many jumps in time don't work.

The timeline begins with my move from Brooklyn to Manhattan. Interspersed are passages of my parents' lives before and during the Holocaust and my childhood. I don't want to restructure, because the work ahead would be enormous. I didn't sign on for Enormous in my fourth attempt to complete a memoir.

I'm stuck. Last week a colleague published his first novel with an impressive publisher. I was jealous. Where's my novel? Where are all my books?

I'm not a real writer.

I should have gone to Iowa.

I should have visited my mother more often.

The road of self-hatred is ugly.

But also inspired. I Googled Bendel's. I discovered their Open See was in one week. I rushed to the trimmings stores, purchased ribbons and velvet and all sorts of crazy colors, and went to work, draping tulle all over my apartment.

This morning. At 4:40 a.m., I was sixteenth on line. We sat on back-packs (me), blankets and chairs (them . . . very smart). Almost everyone was jittery. I was not. I had already done what I needed to do. Show up. Commit to something.

At 9:00, we were taken inside. Suddenly, I was excited. I went to the hair accessories desk. Then the nerves came. I cared, after all. She (the buyer) said my bows were beautiful. Deep sigh. But not right for them (which means time for the memoir . . .).

I was home at 10:20 a.m. and I was glad I went. But I wonder how I would feel if the buyer had wanted my bows. I wonder if that would fill me with anxiety just as the thought of finishing my memoir does.

OUTER EDGES

I filled out applications for rent-stabilized apartments and signed up with a Manhattan realtor (fee). I have mixed feelings (but of course). If an apartment comes through, and then I get a great job offer in say, Prescott, Arizona, what will I do? Face the same awful feeling as when I couldn't say yes to Iowa?

Arghh . . . I did the only thing I could: I went back to Kripalu to soak up that health and sanity. On the bus ride to Lenox, Massachusetts, I sat in front of a woman talking on her cell phone. She was planning a trip to Greece and lots of countries in between. She referred, quite often, to the "outer edges" of the trip. "I'll book the outer edges," she said, "and we'll do the rest later."

I felt jealous of this woman I didn't know, who gave the impression (to eavesdropping me) this was a routine jaunt. Casual enough to plan while on the bus to her home in Stockbridge. I wished the driver would enforce the "no cell phone" sign at the front of the bus. I mused about her phrase "outer edges." It bothered me, and I wasn't sure why. My inner edges, the ones that led me to return to Kripalu, became pointy and sharp.

My green-eyed monster was back. Sometimes I'm so at peace I think I've slain the monster. But a feeling of yearning can well up at any moment, and I forget that the outer edges of anything are often blurry. So many times I've yearned for something I already had.

When I arrived at Kripalu, I settled in and breathed—I took my laptop to the café, booted up, and sent my friend Paul an email. I told him I took a late bus after work and had arrived at 10:00 p.m. It was a treat to myself, I said, paying for the extra night just so I could wake up here—soften my inner edges with 6:30 a.m. yoga. Paul wrote back: *One of the things I admire about you is that you know how to take care of yourself.* That was one of the nicest things anyone had ever said to me. But, of course, Paul wasn't with me when I was on the bus, listening in on someone else's life, having no idea of their internal landscape.

I took a writing workshop with Natalie Goldberg; I did a lot of ten-minute writing, producing the exact same material I've been obsessing over in *Halfway Home*—so much for breaking up with the past. It appears that no matter where I am or when it is, I'm always searching for a way to bring my inner and outer edges closer together.

Mixing It Up

I bought a short-term membership at the Y. Zumba now competes with yoga for my time. The vigorous, lively dance workout stirs fantasies of long ago, when I wanted to be a jazz dancer. In the gym, amidst a tangle of hips, arms, and legs, I catch myself in the mirror and imagine I'm in a Broadway musical, most likely *A Chorus Line*.

The *New York Times* recently had an article on Zumba. I wasn't surprised to note that yoga studios offer these classes, as they require intense focus. In most dance and aerobics classes, the teacher gives verbal cues. In Zumba, the cues are physical. The instructor points left, nods her head forward, claps, draws a circle with her finger above her head. If I escape into myself (or, *when* I escape into myself), it's all over.

I love the Y with its down-home ambience and its menu of classes. It's quite different from the yoga studio I go to, with its Upper East Side patrons who deck the coat hangers with Searle. Lately I've been thinking I should quit the studio and stop being a yoga snob. But then my yoga thinking kicks in, and I remember the physical poses are a small part of the practice.

At the Upper East Side yoga studio I feel cared for and warmed in the small space that is lit by candles and overlooks a garden. Sometimes, right there, where I lay my mat, I find my *drishti* in the center of me.

PEBBLES AND STONES

One of my classes just finished a chapter in *The Things They Carried*. (I never tire of teaching this book.) Jimmy Cross carries a pebble, given to him by a woman he is infatuated with. For Cross, who is in Vietnam, the pebble symbolizes home, Martha, all things pure and light. In contrast, he also carries a stone in his belly—the weight of his guilt when a soldier under his leadership is shot.

The universality of the things we all carry—tangible like the pebble, intangible like guilt—remains in my mind long after the class has finished the novel.

This morning I learned, the awful news about an eight-year-old Orthodox Jewish boy, Leiby Kletzky; he was kidnapped and viciously killed by a neighborhood man. I wished I had been in Borough Park, seen Leiby standing innocently on the sidewalk just before asking a man for directions; I'd have noticed the boy by himself and kept my eye on him. When he walked toward the stranger, I'd have stepped between him and the horror.

That I would be in Borough Park is highly unlikely. But, in my imagining, my cousin, who works in that neighborhood, had called to arrange lunch. What great fortune that I was there, attuned to the lost child.

My rescue fantasy became so real that the stone in my belly dissipated, until I understood where this was all going. My grandfather, killed in the camps, was named Leibich. I had wished as a child to have been his savior—to bring back the lightness to my father that he had carried long ago, before I knew him. The man I knew my father to be was serious, but sometimes he forgot all that weighed him down. His sweet laughter fell to the ground like pebbles to the earth.

My father and all he was and wasn't will always be the things I carry.

WHAT IF?

I went back to work on *Halfway Home*, my editor's notes in hand. I'm conflicted over what to do with what I thought was the book's heart. Her suggestion is to turn it into a work of its own. The section is about my maternal grandparents who left Czechoslovakia with their first two children in 1908; they arrived in Philadelphia by steamship.

My grandfather's inability to find work and tales of American luxuries brought his small family to the land to which almost two million Eastern European Jews had arrived between 1882 and 1924.

Soon after my grandparents arrived, the wealthy cousins who had sponsored their journey found my grandfather a job in the garment trade. I imagine my grandparents settled in South Philadelphia, where 80,000 Jews lived by 1910. Within two years, a child was born there—my aunt Frieda. Shortly thereafter, my grandfather lost his job. The family of five boarded a train for Manhattan and became part of the crush of people in the streets, squeezed between pushcarts and horse-drawn carriages on the Lower East Side.

My Uncle Sam was born in 1913; they were then a family of six. In addition to the crowded and unhealthy conditions, Jewish immigrants were forced to assimilate by working on the Sabbath.

My grandfather, who again worked for a tailor, either lost his job or quit. I imagine that made the family dependant on their cousins. My grandparents were unhappy in New York. They were peasants who'd lived on farms. On the Lower East Side, families were squeezed together in two rooms with poor or no ventilation. There was one bathroom for two families. A workday could last from 7:00 a.m. to 10:00 p.m.

The family missed Czechoslovakia, and the cousins resented their immigrant relatives with their satchels of belongings, hungry children, and guttural Yiddish tongue.

The cousins put up the funds to pay for my grandparents' passage back across the Atlantic with their children. One in twenty Jewish immigrants returned disenchanted to Europe in 1915. My family was among them.

Knowing that they had traded one uncertain fate for another is eerie, unsettling.

Four more children were born. My grandparents died before the Nazis invaded their homeland. Sam and Frieda were U.S. citizens and able to leave; six children had to face what would come to Eastern European Jews.

I thought this story was the heart of the book, because I see myself in my grandparents' choices. They reached for a better life, and then returned to the life they knew. Their circumstances were harsh in a way mine aren't. But the undertow seems the same, the deep pull back to familial land. The theme that runs through my brain now is "so near and yet so far."

The anecdote about my grandparents' journey was told to me when I was old enough to understand the implications. I recall the "what if" feeling I had. What if my mother had been born in America? Would she have met my father, somehow, and still had me? A very big "what if." How much wider our boundaries might have been.

Would luck and happiness then have molded her (and therefore, me) into natural yes people? Then again, is luck 50 percent perception? After all, my mother and her five siblings survived the camps—what amazing luck that was! And who knows? Perhaps if they'd stayed in

America, one of them would have been hit by a Ford Roadster while crossing a street.

Everything happens for a reason, my mother often said. I never believed it except for the cause and effect of life. But I was glad my mother believed it; I was glad for everything that helped her accept her present moments.

Putting It All to Bed

In the newsroom, when an article is completed, journalists use the phrase "put the story to bed." That phrase comes to me as I send my six-page essay "The Ambivalent Memoirist" to *Poets & Writers*.

I've been at Starbucks for two hours. Neighbors stream in and out. They stop at my table to say hi. They watch my laptop while I go to the bathroom. I love how Midtown can feel like a small town. Yet, in spite of all this neighborliness, while browsing for apartments on the Internet, I want to live everywhere! I have a friend in Charlotte. I Google "Charlotte NC apartments." Voila! So many with terraces, swimming pools, tennis courts. I don't know anyone in Santa Fe, but so what?

I log onto www.apartments.com and search for Nyack. There are apartments in two-family houses and above stores for under $1,400. My heart expands. I send the link to myself to read when I'm home.

One last hit: I Google "Teach English in Tbilisi." Someday soon I will download an application.

History of a Move

I called a broker (fee) and went up to Nyack to see the apartments. The one above a store is near a bar and the two-family is really an attic (illegal, not to mention Anne Frank analogies). A third apartment in a small complex was on the ground floor, two rooms with windows facing a brick wall. I thought I could do better rent-wise in Nyack—but it doesn't seem cheaper than Manhattan, plus the fee for a broker.

The plusses of moving there? Mesmerizing views of the Hudson, quiet lifestyle but with yoga (a lot of yoga), artsy shops and cafes, lovely bus ride to and from Manhattan—not counting the traffic, Lincoln Tunnel, and Port Authority. Biggest plus? It's the unknown and away-ish and new.

On the bus ride home, I wondered, *After I settle into my apartment, take a walk, find a yoga studio I like, fill the cupboards—what will I do?* I felt a startling sense of displacement. This memory came to mind: Many years ago I saw the documentary *Punch Me in the Stomach*, by Deb Filler. In this film, which Filler wrote and starred in, she presents her father's story of being rounded up and taken to Auschwitz. In a scene I can never forget, Filler (as her father) tells how he and the other Jews were given their uniforms then told to lie down. The cots were set up in fours—two pushed together sideways, up against two cots, foot to foot. *There we were, taken from our homes, to lay on these cots waiting for what they would tell us to do next. We lay down, and we looked at each other. All we could do was laugh.*

People in the midst of productive lives of working and caring for families were pulled from those lives, put into pajamas, and instructed, like children, to lie down. It was crazy.

Moving from Manhattan to Nyack is not even remotely like the scene Filler depicts. Yet, I feel stranded, lost, and think of Auschwitz.

Getting Closer

E ight weeks from now is my must-move-by deadline.

Manhattan is so here, so forgiving of my wishy-washy affections. Manhattan is my perfect husband, loving me unconditionally, my best friend who is never too busy for me. Manhattan is my Saturday night date, my Sunday walk in the park.

Do I want to break up and have a fling with another city?

I received a letter about a rent-stabilized apartment in Manhattan. There are parameters I have to meet and papers to get together—lots of papers.

Not Yet Home

In the college adjunct office, I tooled around on Craigslist and found a Nyack house sublet. Affordable? Check. Location? Check. Cuteness factor? From the description . . . check. Adventure? Check!

I sent an email and heard back immediately—my future and possible landlord is moving to Manhattan (but, of course), and will use her Nyack house occasionally. Most of the time it will be all mine.

Maybe it was some sort of test: me, standing in the middle of two opposing options. A house rental I could afford where I wasn't comfortable (not to mention made me think of Auschwitz) versus the possibility of an apartment I could afford in the place I'm comfortable. Plan A. Plan B.

Iowa Tucson Albuquerque Pittsburgh. Manhattan.

Write a novel with a book packager and possibly make millions or write a novel on my own (like most people) and who knows?

I took the bus up to Nyack to see the house. It was a half mile from Main Street, the main drag; in winter without a car, getting to yoga and cafés would be hard, but I was told cabs were inexpensive. The landlord was out of town; her friend who lived nearby showed me the house. It wasn't the charming cottage with a front deck, as I'd pictured. I felt distant and awkward, yet unable to say flat-out that it wasn't the right place for me.

What Is Ordained

One of my fiction classes is beginning Hosseini's *A Thousand Splendid Suns*. In this story set in Afghanistan, Mariam and Laila are two women who form a deep tie, in spite of being born into different life expectations.

If I were to say which woman I most identify with, I'd say Mariam. She accepts her fate of a loveless and abusive marriage. She hides her unhappiness behind a burka, where she ultimately finds comfort. Mariam's outer life is not mine, of course. I have freedom, am educated, am not abused. It is her acceptance of her limits that rings true for me—she learns to live within the confines of the black fabric that covers her.

Every woman would want to be a Laila—beautiful, spirited, educated, loved. Laila welcomes life and love because those gifts were ordained for her. When circumstances seem to put a harrowing end to Laila's dreams, she finds what she needs, within life's new terms.

I fell asleep last night thinking about these two women, aware that somewhere in their combined stories is mine. My present conflict isn't close to the hardships of Mariam and Laila; to compare us is perhaps disrespectful. Except that we are fighting wars. Theirs is present tense, mine in a past that pushes its way into my present.

What are the "new terms" within which I can find happiness? Do I have to leave all I know to find it?

STILL NOT HOME

The Nyack possible-future landlord emails. She is coming into Manhattan. Can we meet to discuss going forward? Several friends say the Nyack situation isn't good. They say I'll be lonely, will have no places to walk to, and without a car, how will I get food? (One day soon, I will stop asking friends what they think.)

In spite of not having liked the house (and my anticipation/worry that a rent-stabilized apartment will come through), I email back, *Yes, let's meet*. Actually, I write, *Yes!* (And that is for the book packager and all the schools I didn't go away to and so much more.) I call Laura and tell her I'll be moving in four weeks, and I'd like to sell all my furnishings, dishes, all of it. I tell her, "Please ask Amy if she wants anything."

Do or Die

My future landlord and I meet over coffee. She's fortyish, pretty and dressed as I am in jeans and sweater. After quick look-overs, we relax. She's nice and normal and after some basic chitchat (she'll drive me to Costco so I can fill the cupboards), she guesses the exact shade of lipstick I'm wearing (MAC's O). When it's time to sign an agreement (which I wrote in case she didn't—she didn't), she says, "I raised the cost of electricity from $50 to $100; with the dishwasher, heat, television, $100 isn't even enough."

While absorbing this information, she says, the agreement I wrote up won't work. "We need a roommate agreement," she says. "I'm going to come home on weekends. There are two bedrooms. You can have whichever one you want."

Still absorbing, I'm aware of the collision of thoughts in my mind. *She is my get-out-of-New York card. But, this doesn't feel right. I don't want a roommate—or do I? She has a car. She mentioned Costco . . . she knew my lipstick . . .*

She says she'll email me an agreement. I say, "Okay."

Getting Honest

I walk home slowly down First Avenue and stop for a slice of pizza, suddenly ravenous. Biting into the perfect, thin crust, my gut *finally* has words with me: *I don't care if she is a lipstick genius. Don't do it.*

FIGHTING WITH GHOSTS

I dream of moving across the world to Tbilisi, the country to Tucson, landing on a mountaintop in Taos (after flying in to Albuquerque). I wake up and Google "Tbilisi Yoga" "Tucson Yoga" "Pittsburgh Yoga" and this is an oh-my-God moment, because Donna Farhi, my favorite yoga writer, teaches in a studio there.

I torture myself. "Ambivalent Memoirist" is merely one tip of my yes-no story

"Trust your gut," people say. "Trust your instincts." My gut and my instincts are getting closer. I'm not moving to Nyack. I *am* moving to a short-term furnished sublet I found in a day because Amy is moving in, and I must go someplace. I tell you this shamefully: the apartment I'm moving to is around the corner and "up the hill" above First Avenue on Tudor City Place.

I pick up my pen to see if it will tell me how I got here, almost exactly where I was when I began my flight from the constraints of sameness.

It began with a cream-colored '93 Buick.

An October day in 1994; my parents loaded their car with forty-seven years of belongings and memories of their Brooklyn lives. My mother wore her kerchief to protect her ears from the draft as they drove to their home

in Florida. She wore large sunglasses to shield her from the sun and cover her tears.

Then, the car didn't start. My mother saw that as an omen that mirrored all her anxieties and doubts of leaving her children, her siblings, all that was the Brooklyn she loved. My father called AAA, then waited outside. My mother called me. Maybe we shouldn't go. Tell me, sweetheart. What do you think? I wasn't the best person for her to ask, for I looked forward to the literal distance the move would provide us. And so I urged her on, assuring her she would be okay.

AAA arrived; the car started. My parents took off for a thirty-six-hour drive. On the way down, my mother had four small heart attacks, tiny blip blips that she thought was indigestion. She called me from the hospital and left a message on my answer machine: "It's Mommy. I had heart failure."

My mother's life in Florida was punctuated by a series of hospitalizations. My life in Brooklyn was stunted by the messages that awaited me. My mother lived for another nine years. To say it was the move that killed her would not be hyperbole. The move from Brooklyn to Florida represented a forward leap into the future—for her and, to the best of my ability, for me. Both of those leaps were a loss for my mother of all she knew and loved.

I am fighting ghosts.

THE POWER OF STORIES

I'm in my interim Tudor City apartment, getting ready for the summer semester. I'm again with O'Brien's words, in the center of him and myself.

A few lines I love: "Stories are for joining the past to the future. Stories are for those late hours in the night when you can't remember how you got from where you were to where you are." These sentences remind me of a story my father often told.

There was a small village in Czechoslovakia. Everyone had terrible problems. One man was a cripple and couldn't walk without a cane in each hand; a woman cried that her husband couldn't make a living; everyone was poor; a mother said her daughter couldn't find a husband, the family was shamed; a man's son didn't want to learn Talmud, this was unheard of.

The rabbi in the village gathered everyone in a circle. He said, "Throw your problems into the center. Go ahead. Give away your troubles." Everyone walked into the middle, they pretended they held in their hands giant rocks. Just like on Yom Kippur, for tashlich, when we throw away our sins. They put down the "rocks." They went back to the circle.

The rabbi said, "Now, go take the problem that is easier. Any one you choose." They went back; they stood for a few minutes scratching their heads, doing nothing. Then one by one, they took back their own problems. You see, Símala, whatever is yours is easier to face than what is someone else's.

My father's understanding of that story was not simply that the known is better than the unknown. He wanted me to be at peace with my life and its complicated mix of problems and happiness.

My friend Diane went to Tbilisi because that's where her career in public policy took her. My neighbor worked for the United Nations, and she was called to Kenya. Where does my life call me?

Timing Is Everything

I'm comfortable in my 250-square foot temporary quarters. All I own here is packed in boxes—clothes, books, CDs, mementoes, and assorted necessities like printer and personal items. Amy bought all my stuff.

I like being in a holding pattern. I'm in transit, but not there yet. Days and weeks go by in which I marvel that I've now lived in two Manhattan apartments! At work, I still do apartment searches. One teacher, for whom moving was an easy choice from the East Village to Astoria, shakes his head. *You still haven't found a place?*

And that's when the phone call comes to tell me there's a rent-stabilized apartment available. It's a four-hundred-square-foot studio on the edge of Chelsea. I'm nervous, confused, completely disconnected from what I want.

The next day I go there with Laurie. I can't help but worry, *What if I don't like it? What if I do like it?*

I don't know what I expected—to look out the window and feel as if I were at the foot of those glorious Taos mountains? Out the windows is a courtyard; it's quiet and peaceful. *This is a good apartment*, Laurie says. And, it is. Of course, I want it; but I want something else too—to pass the test I had given myself. To climb to the top of something and be *there*. Even though it seems that what I want and need are a totally different kind of climb.

FINALLY

I was glad to leave Tudor City, quite likely because I was never fully there. Neither of my sublets felt like mine. But then, that had been the point: to never get stuck again for twenty-seven years.

I was planning on taking a cab to my new apartment, but the movers told me to ride shotgun in the front seat. Seated between them in the van, I wanted to be on the road forever. I imagined us heading down U.S. 1 and past signs to Monterey, Santa Barbara, Palos Verdes. (Have I not mentioned California in my palette of places to go?)

We wound our way through traffic, turned left, away from the cars that headed to the Lincoln Tunnel and disappeared in the snaky darkness.

ABOUT A MOVE

For a few days, I was without Internet access. The writing I did was akin to my early days at the computer—all my energy was funneled into Microsoft Word, not Holy Google. Now, I'm hooked up (so to speak) and read blogs and fiddle around on the Net. Then I run out for an iced coffee and feel the tremor of anxiety. I'm not as far as I'd "tried" to get, yet the effort to adapt to where I am feels unwieldy.

I'm only a mile away from Tudor City. Many people who know me say they're not surprised I stayed close to home. Most likely, they think of my past experiences with choices, moves, risks. They don't consider the complexities I travel with, the experiences that shape my idiosyncratic self.

What I do know is this: the distance doesn't always matter; it's all new, regardless. When I leave my apartment, I try to remember: Keys? Sunglasses? Wallet? Where are my new places for these things?

My father hated his move to assisted living. As much as I thought I understood his feelings—I see now, that I couldn't possibly. He missed the large things, yes, especially the incline on the sofa where my mother once sat. But my father also missed the small things. His familiar teacup near the stove, the drawer where he kept his papers (and he had so many papers), the table that held his yarmulke and reading glasses.

On my third day in Chelsea, I took a class at the Iyengar Studio on West 23rd. The precise, slow movements opened me up, brought yoga back into my body. At home, a swell of emotion poured out, and I sobbed. At first I thought my grief was for the loss of my neighbors, the familiar East Side streets, my Starbucks home; but the intensity lingered, and here's where this is headed:

This is the first apartment I've settled into for real, with neither of my parents alive. There isn't a new address I will give them, and, of course, assurances that the neighborhood is safe, there are grocery stores nearby. Their phone calls will never reach here. If by some crazy miracle they were to return to life, say, for an hour, and wanted to use that hour to pay me a visit, they wouldn't know where to look for me.

RETURN TO THE BODY

L ast night I tried another yoga class in my new neighborhood. The Kripalu-trained teacher began with a quotation I found much solace in:

"Every time you judge yourself, you break your own heart . . . Do not fight the dark, just turn on the light, and breathe into the goodness that you are." (Swami Kripalu)

What those words meant to me was to not feel shame over my choices, even in moments when I feel disappointed with myself. "Do not fight the dark." These words tell me, each time I wish to be elsewhere, I'm blind to the possibilities of my own life.

Can I brighten my choice to stay in Manhattan? The answer lies in yoga. That's what my body told me when I woke up this morning feeling wonderful. I felt every bit of my physical self. My arms and legs and heart and lungs and all of me beyond my brain want to be in on my life. I can't move through the world through mere thought. I must take actions, engage, go outside. Yoga, life, insist upon it.

FYI, *Poets & Writers* rejected "The Ambivalent Memoirist" and wrote, *You should have no trouble placing it.* That's what's known in my trade as "a good rejection."

Settling In

My new desk arrived, and I found my writing space in front of the window that overlooks the courtyard. Tall buildings surround the open area, and one naked tree, still recovering from winter, is directly in my view. Every day more pink buds appear. *I'm watching you*, I say to the tree. It's my new bridge, except it's not a horizontal extension that will take me to another place.

The idea and thrill and fear of moving has not gone away, but I'm seated at a different angle. Will the commotion inside of me settle? Will I ordain to myself the ability to just live?

I'm into pink. So little-girlish. And yet, it is not the little girl in me I'm feeding, with my pale pink plates and coffee mug and pink sheets. I'm experimenting with colors—out with the earth tones that dominated my decorating tastes since 1970. I bought a deep-red loveseat and blue bowls, and delight at the sight of my purple/pink/blue bathroom.

Manhattan streets provide traction to my day. I run here and there. Find new coffee homes, cute places. My few pieces of furniture fall into a perfect arrangement. Then I move everything around.

REEVALUATING

I applied for a full-time lectureship at one of the schools where I adjunct. I knew I would be one of hundreds of adjuncts—equally qualified, just as earnest—and with grammatically perfect cover letters. I didn't want to want that job too much—I knew the chances, knew my own ambivalence (settling into a big-city college, a schedule of all composition classes)—but truth be told, when I survived the first round of rejections, I got excited.

I imagined my cubbyhole of an office, my friends visiting, my incredibly high self-esteem from being a full-time lecturer. I grew taller, filled myself out. I carried that image—which became a belief—into my classes. I was a better teacher.

A second round of rejection letters went out . . . I hadn't received one. I imagined further—a perfect symmetry of work and home? New apartment new job? *I am* in the right place!? Yesterday, the letter found its way to my new address. I wasn't disappointed—not at first; although I was surprised because I had come to feel . . . well, that I deserved that job.

But a few hours after reading the letter, I felt smaller. My office had been taken away, and I had rejoined the masses. I hadn't even realized until that moment, that I felt small in my patchwork of teaching jobs.

Ah . . . a big yes! Four weeks later I asked for and received a promotion at the college that is part of CUNY; I went from adjunct lecturer to adjunct assistant professor. *That* letter in the mail filled me with joy.

FYI, I don't want to be a yoga teacher, but I *do* want to instinctively know better than to let a job define me, whether I get it or not.

Some Time Away

It's day four of a weeklong teacher's conference at Bard Institute for Writing and Thinking. Seated in front of a picture window, I look out through a bramble of branches and leaves, mountains of trees. Early afternoon, I'll take the Metro-North back to Manhattan to teach my 5:30 class. I'll sleep in my own bed (I miss my new apartment!), and then return to this campus for three more days to nourish my intellect and still my yearning for a country place.

Now I write through a hazy feeling of wakefulness—a smooth, settled peace of mind, not yet ready for the world. In this life—this Rhinecliff, New York, conference-y life—the world, when it enters, will not be the crush of the city. The world will quietly take its seats, smile sleepily, open notebooks, and write.

My walk to the dining hall for my first cup of coffee, which I sip while sitting on a bench close to squirrels and birds, is a lovely way to start my day. And in all this present-moment loveliness, I drift, returning to the common dialogue that is my brain. *Is this what my life would have looked like had I gone to Iowa Tucson Albuquerque (most likely, not Pittsburgh)?*

Sprawling college campuses provide a fertile ground for my mind to wander (and wonder). Participants reminisce about their college days—this city, that one, then graduation and a leap to another city and another. My high school friends and I were rooted to the Brooklyn earth, our parents' visions of where we belonged when we went to college.

We were the offspring of working-class parents, some educated, some not, at least 50 percent immigrants, making a life of hard knocks and ordinary choices. They didn't know about places like Bard, Vassar, Berkeley (*we* barely did). We went from college (in Brooklyn) to marriage to lives as mini grown-ups. Then mini explosions in most of our lives as the marriages ended, playing-house time was up, and the world of choice came along.

On Bard's campus, I seek to fill that eighteen-year-old girl in me who wants four years of preparation for life, four years to experiment, learn, and commune with knowledge and love away from my parents' gaze.

I imagine hiding out here for a month or two (or three), finishing *Halfway Home*, burrowing into memories that seem sharper away from the city of my birth. Maybe by the time I'm finished, the Brooklyn girl I write about will seem to me like an intriguing artifact.

Now, the clamor of footsteps approaching. Class will soon begin. We'll take out our notebooks, click our pens, write something.

Early Morning Musings

I awake at 5:00 a.m., in tune with the outside world, which is a hush of air through my window. By 7:00 a.m. on weekdays, garbage trucks are at work. My neighbors describe the sound as deafening; for me it is a whisper, not nearly like the clanking, honking, and gusto of East 42nd Street. From fourteen floors above, I often dialed 311, the city's complaint phone number, about ConEd's midnight drilling, the infernal rumble of cars over street plates. Others dialed 311 begging to put a stop to drunken revelers at the corner bar.

This Brooklyn girl from modest means had certain life expectations. One of them was not that I would live on East 42nd Street, in the center of the world.

The thing about living in the center of the world is that it wasn't always my own life I was in the middle of.

OVERLOAD

L ast night I was greeted by students groaning about the assignment: *tedious, took three hours to do, I didn't understand it,* and
variations on the theme.

At Bard, I learned that when students don't understand, that's not
necessarily bad. During my own week of learning, when the teacher
gave a prompt, we all did something, whether we understood or not.
Pen to paper . . . that was the credo.

I want to believe that in my students' cases, not understanding
was part of the learning process. But, in truth, I'd hurried the assignment and was embarrassed when it fell apart. During the next class, we
plowed through for an hour and dismantled the dense text.

KISS THE GROUND

There is a twenty-foot-by-twenty-foot street plate on my corner, creating a huge amount of traffic noise. Not to mention major drilling, digging, honking. I haven't seen or heard anything like it since my defection across town. Mercifully, my apartment doesn't face the street. Sitting in front of my computer, I hear only the din of the TV, occasional murmurs outside my door, and the morning rumble of garbage trucks.

I went to D.C. for the weekend, loved every second of walking around Dupont Circle, past the Potomac River, and exploring Kramerbooks and vintage clothing stores. Yet, I couldn't wait to get home—my home, my bed, my this, my that. I pictured myself kissing the floors. There's a phrase that comes to me from a favorite essay, "A Pen by the Phone" by Debra Anne Davis. In describing her father, she reflects on how little it took for him to feel content with his life. She writes, ". . . peace comes unbidden if we prepare a small space and a little time to receive it."

I roll down my bedspread, puff up the pillows, then stand back, gaze at the bounty of my home. Outside my windows, sun reflects on the fire escapes and the tree that is now thick with late summer leaves.

In my mind I write: *unbidden is such a lovely word.*

RETURN TO THE PAGE

This morning I walked to Hudson Yards, a neighborhood around Tenth Avenue and the West 30s, which I've taken a strong liking to. It's a bit of a walk from home, but with my laptop in a shoulder bag and plans to write at the Café Grind (my new favorite place), it's a walk I love. En route, I imagined blogging while looking out on a gas station and a Dunkin' Donuts that's seen better days. I imagined plumbing the whys and whats that compel me to this area that is rife with parking lots, truck traffic, and massive apartment buildings.

There's the away-ness of it—the feeling I often search for and that does my writing life well. Alas, the Café Grind was closed for Labor Day weekend and so, here I sit, settled in at Argo Tea a few blocks from home, with an iced cappuccino. (Maybe that's why I'm in Manhattan, where I can get almost anything, including coffee in a tea place.) The away-ness of Hudson Yards is replaced with people traffic instead of trucks. The outdoor lunch van is already setting up. Yellow cabs dart down Seventh Avenue. The city is awake.

I read an article this week in *Yoga Journal* about the brain having a default setting. My interpretation is that when I stop the activities that comprise my day, my brain is no longer busy, helping me get things done. And so it returns to its usual lament, which is to yearn.

Home—An Epilogue

The question *What next?* rises up and I want to push it back. I don't know what's next and don't know if something has to be next.

My colleague who is publishing his novel with an impressive publisher says I should develop my fiction. He says to make none of it autobiographical, then my writing life will be peaceful. How lovely that would be . . . but is a writing life, or just plain life, supposed to be peaceful?

Last night I was an hour early for my yoga class. I asked the yogi at the front desk if I could borrow a pen and a scrap of paper. I lit up inside because I felt new to writing, to this gift so readily available here, but not yet in my apartment. I scribbled across the page. By the time class started, I had two pages and wasn't done. A character fell out of my spleen:

On Monday morning Janine will be across the river, in one of those beckoning buildings. She will tell everyone at work she is moving to Manhattan. "But Brooklyn is so cool," they will say. She will smile to herself, not bother to explain. Hope and possibilities will frame Janine's new life. Greatness will be hers for the taking.

I'll leave soon for yoga class and be early again. Maybe I'll learn more about Janine. Perhaps my words will wander. I'll put pen to paper, begin, end up anywhere or everywhere.

7509773R00134

Made in the USA
San Bernardino, CA
09 January 2014